Groovy Programming Language for Automation

Unlock the full potential of Groovy to streamline workflows, simplify coding

Davis Simon

1

Discover Other Books in the Series

"Groovy Programming Language for Beginners: Your First Steps into Coding"

"Groovy Programming Language for Backend Development:Discover How Groovy Can Revolutionize Your Backend Code"

"Groovy Programming language for Chatbots:The Ultimate Guide to Building Intelligent Chatbots with Ease"

"Groovy Programming Language for Data Science: Unlock the Power of Seamless Data Analysis and Automation"

"Groovy Programming Language for Web Development: Building Your First Web App"

"Groovy Programming Language for Big Data:Groovy to Build Scalable, Efficient, and Flexible Big Data Applications"

"Groovy Programming Language for Data Manipulation: Master the Basics and Unlock Advanced Techniques for Game-Changing Results"

"Groovy Programming Language for DevSecOps: Agile Scripting to Secure and Streamline Software Delivery With Groovy"

Disclaimer

The Book titled *"Groovy Programming Language for Automation: Unlock the full potential of Groovy to streamline workflows, simplify coding"* by Davis Simon is intended for educational and informational purposes only.

The content provided in this Book is based on the author's experience, research, and personal opinions. It is designed to offer insights and techniques for backend development using the Groovy programming language.

Introduction

Welcome to **"Groovy Programming Language for Automation"**—your all-encompassing resource for leveraging the capabilities of Groovy to enhance and optimize your workflows. In the current fast-evolving digital landscape, automation has transitioned from being a mere advantage to an essential requirement. Both businesses and developers are in pursuit of more effective methods to handle repetitive tasks, boost productivity, and minimize errors. Groovy, a dynamic language that operates on the Java platform, presents an ideal solution.

This book caters to both novices and seasoned programmers eager to explore the extensive possibilities that Groovy offers. With its streamlined syntax and effortless compatibility with existing Java libraries, Groovy simplifies the automation of routine tasks. Throughout this text, you will learn how Groovy can ease the coding process, enabling you to concentrate on achieving results rather than becoming entangled in intricate syntax and lengthy code.

We will begin with the basics of Groovy, examining its syntax, features, and integration with various tools and technologies. You will discover the distinctive attributes that differentiate Groovy, including its robust closures, dynamic typing, and inherent support for functional programming. As we advance, we will investigate practical applications, demonstrating how Groovy can be employed to enhance workflows across different fields—be it testing, deployment, or data processing.

By the conclusion of this book, you will possess not only a strong grounding in Groovy programming but also a repertoire of techniques and best practices for implementing automation solutions tailored to your unique requirements. This is more than just a technical guide; it serves as a pathway to unlocking innovation and efficiency through automation.Join us on this journey to discover how the Groovy programming language can revolutionize the way you work. Let's unlock its full potential together and take your automation skills to new heights!

Chapter 1: Introduction to Groovy for Automation

Organizations are continually seeking methods to optimize their processes, reduce human error, and enhance overall efficiency. Automation has emerged as a pivotal solution to address these issues, with Groovy recognized as a prominent programming language that supports automation due to its ease of use, flexibility, and robust features. This chapter offers an introductory overview of Groovy as an essential tool for automation, laying the groundwork for a more in-depth examination in the following chapters.

1.1 What is Groovy?

Groovy is a dynamic and agile programming language that operates on the Java Virtual Machine (JVM). It enriches the Java platform with advanced scripting capabilities while ensuring compatibility with existing Java code. Created by James Strachan and introduced in 2003, Groovy has gained popularity across various applications, particularly in automation, web development, and testing.### 1.1.1 Key Features of Groovy

Ease of Use: Groovy's syntax is intuitive and concise, making it easier for both beginners and experienced developers to write and understand code. This reduces the learning curve associated with automation tasks.

Static and Dynamic Typing: Groovy supports both static and dynamic typing, providing flexibility in coding. Developers can write scripts quickly without the need for verbose type declarations, but can also leverage static typing when type safety is a priority.

Seamless Java Integration: Since Groovy runs on the JVM, it integrates seamlessly with Java libraries and frameworks. This allows for the reuse of existing Java code and the ability to access Java libraries, significantly expanding Groovy's capabilities.

Rich Ecosystem: Groovy comes with a variety of libraries and tools, such as Grails for web development and Spock for testing. Its compatibility with other Java frameworks further enhances its appeal in automation.

1.2 Why Use Groovy for Automation?

Automation scripts can be written in many programming languages, but Groovy's unique advantages make it particularly suitable for numerous automation scenarios.

1.2.1 Concise and Readable Code

In automation, readability is crucial. Automation scripts are often maintained by different people over time, so code clarity can save significant amounts of time and effort. Groovy's syntax allows developers to express complex logic in fewer lines of code, enhancing clarity and maintainability.

1.2.2 Versatility in Scripting and Integration

Groovy is not limited to a specific type of automation; it can be employed for scripting tasks, automating builds, testing applications, or orchestrating workflows. Additionally, it integrates smoothly with popular tools such as Jenkins for CI/CD, enabling automated builds and deployments with ease.

1.2.3 Enhanced Testing Capabilities

Writing automated tests is a critical part of the development process. Groovy's resemblance to Java allows developers to utilize existing testing frameworks like JUnit, while the Spock framework, developed specifically for Groovy, offers a powerful and expressive way to write tests, particularly for behavior-driven development.

1.2.4 Community and Support

Groovy has a vibrant community that contributes a wealth of libraries, documentation, and forums. This community support means that developers can find resources, troubleshoot issues, and share best practices, making Groovy a practical choice for organizations looking to implement automation widely.

1.3 Getting Started with Groovy

To begin using Groovy for automation, you will need to set up your environment. The installation process is straightforward:

Install Java: Since Groovy runs on the JVM, ensuring you have the latest version of the Java Development Kit (JDK) installed is essential.

Install Groovy: You can download the Groovy binaries from the official Groovy website or use package managers like SDKMAN! or Homebrew (for Mac users) to manage your Groovy installation conveniently.

Set Up Your IDE: While Groovy scripts can be run from the command line, using an Integrated Development Environment (IDE) like IntelliJ IDEA or Eclipse enhances productivity with advanced features such as code completion, debugging, and integrated testing tools.

After successfully setting up your environment, you can write your first Groovy script. A simple "Hello, World!" example would look like this:

```groovy
println 'Hello, World!'
```

Running this script in the Groovy command line will display "Hello, World!"—a straightforward demonstration of Groovy's syntax.

This chapter provided a foundation for understanding Groovy as a scripting language tailored for automation tasks. We explored what Groovy is, its key features, and the reasons why it is a powerful tool for automation projects. As you proceed through this book, you will uncover in-depth tutorials, examples, and best practices that will enable you to leverage Groovy effectively in your automation workflows.

The Power Groovy for Automation

As organizations strive for efficiency and agility, automation emerges as a powerful ally. Among the myriad of programming languages and scripting tools available, Groovy stands out as a versatile and effective choice for automation tasks. This chapter explores the power of Groovy for automation, highlighting its features, benefits, and practical applications.

1. Introduction to Groovy

Groovy is an agile and dynamic language for the Java Virtual Machine (JVM) that is both syntactically and semantically similar to Java. It enhances Java by introducing scripting capabilities, closures, and a concise syntax, making it a powerful tool for automating tasks and enhancing productivity. Groovy can be integrated seamlessly with existing Java code and libraries, allowing developers to utilize familiar Java frameworks while enjoying the benefits of a more expressive language.

2. Why Choose Groovy for Automation? ### 2.1. Simplicity and Readability

One of Groovy's most significant advantages is its simple and expressive syntax. Unlike some other scripting languages, Groovy reduces boilerplate code significantly, allowing developers to focus on the logic of automation tasks rather than the intricacies of language syntax. This simplicity makes Groovy an excellent choice for both novice programmers and experienced developers looking to streamline their automation processes.

2.2. Native Support for Java Libraries

Since Groovy runs on the JVM, it can easily leverage all the Java libraries and frameworks. This means that developers can write Groovy scripts to perform automation while still accessing a vast ecosystem of existing Java tools. Whether it's using Apache Commons for file manipulation or Spring framework for application integration, Groovy allows developers to tap into the rich resources of the Java ecosystem.

2.3. Domain-Specific Language (DSL) Creation

Groovy's flexibility allows developers to create Domain-Specific Languages (DSLs) tailored to specific automation tasks or processes. A DSL can express solutions in a way that closely mimics natural language, making scripts easier to understand and maintain. This feature is particularly beneficial in environments where collaboration between technical and non-technical stakeholders is essential.

2.4. Excellent Integration Capabilities

Groovy is designed for integration. It can work seamlessly with build systems like Gradle, CI/CD tools like Jenkins, and configuration management tools like Ansible. Automating deployment processes, running tests, and orchestrating various tools become easier when leveraging Groovy's capabilities to connect with other systems.

3. Key Features of Groovy

To fully appreciate the power of Groovy for automation, it's essential to understand its key features. ### 3.1. Closures

Closures are blocks of code that can be executed at a later time. They allow for creating more modular, reusable, and testable code. In automation scripts, closures can encapsulate tasks that can be executed on demand, making it easier to define behavior that can be reused across various automation flows.

3.2. Metaprogramming

Groovy offers powerful metaprogramming capabilities, allowing developers to modify classes and methods at runtime. This feature helps in writing more flexible and dynamic automation scripts where behavior can be altered based on runtime conditions or configuration.

3.3. Built-in Support for XML and JSON

Automating tasks often requires interaction with data formats like XML or JSON. Groovy comes with built- in support for these formats, making parsing and manipulating data straightforward. This allows for simple integration with APIs or configuration files essential for many automation tasks.

4. Practical Applications of Groovy in Automation ### 4.1. Scripted Build Automation

With tools like Jenkins leveraging Groovy, developers can automate their build processes. Groovy scripts can be used to configure jobs, manage build pipelines, and execute test cases. This integration of Groovy into CI/CD pipelines enhances productivity and minimizes manual intervention.

4.2. Configuration Management

Groovy's ability to read and manipulate configuration files allows it to play a vital role in configuration management. Automating the setup and maintenance of environments can be accomplished using Groovy scripts that read, modify, and apply configurations across systems.

4.3. Data Transformation and ETL Processes

ETL (Extract, Transform, Load) processes are common in data engineering. Groovy can be utilized to create lightweight ETL pipelines that extract data from various sources, transform it according to business rules, and load it into target systems. Its support for both XML and JSON makes it an excellent choice for such tasks.

4.4. Testing Automation

Groovy is not only a great choice for building automation scripts but also for testing. Using frameworks like Spock, developers can write concise and expressive tests that leverage Groovy's capabilities to ensure that their code functions correctly. This not only provides confidence in the software but also enhances the overall automation ecosystem.

By leveraging the strengths of Groovy, developers can build efficient, maintainable, and highly productive automation frameworks that meet the demands of a rapidly changing technological landscape. As we move forward, embracing Groovy in our automation toolkit will prepare us for the challenges and opportunities that lie ahead.

Setting Up Your Development Environment

Groovy, a dynamic language for the Java platform, is gaining traction for writing scripts and automation tasks, especially in Continuous Integration/Continuous Deployment (CI/CD) pipelines. In this chapter, we will guide you through the steps required to set up your development environment specifically for Groovy automation.

Understanding Groovy

Before diving into the setup process, it's essential to understand why Groovy is a good choice for automation tasks. Groovy is designed to be intuitive and easy to learn for Java developers, offering excellent interoperability with Java libraries. Moreover, it supports scripting, domain-specific languages, and a variety of programming paradigms, making it flexible for automation needs.

Prerequisites

Before you can start using Groovy for automation, ensure that you have the following installed on your machine:

Java Development Kit (JDK): Groovy runs on the Java Virtual Machine (JVM), so having the correct version of the JDK is crucial. At the time of writing, Groovy supports JDK 8 and later versions.

Groovy: You'll need to install Groovy itself. The recommended version will be the latest stable release, but compatibility with existing projects may dictate your choice.

Integrated Development Environment (IDE): While you can use any text editor to write Groovy scripts, an IDE with Groovy support can significantly enhance your productivity.

Build Tools: Familiarity with tools like Gradle or Maven is helpful, especially for managing dependencies and building automation tasks.

Step-by-Step Environment Setup ### Step 1: Install JDK

Download JDK: Go to the [Oracle JDK download page](https://www.oracle.com/java/technologies/javase-jdk11-downloads.html) or consider using OpenJDK from [AdoptOpenJDK](https://adoptopenjdk.net).

Install JDK: Follow the instructions applicable to your operating system (Windows, macOS, or Linux).

Set JAVA_HOME: After installation, configure the environment variable `JAVA_HOME` to point to your JDK installation directory and add the `bin` directory to your `PATH`.

Step 2: Install Groovy

Download Groovy: Navigate to the [Groovy download page](https://groovy- lang.org/download.html).

*Install Groovy**: Extract the downloaded file to your preferred directory. You can also consider using package managers like SDKMAN! on Unix-based systems or Scoop for Windows to manage your Groovy installation.

Set GROOVY_HOME: Like `JAVA_HOME`, you should also set the `GROOVY_HOME` environment variable to point to your Groovy installation and update your `PATH`.

Step 3: Verify Installations

After completing the installations, verify them by opening a terminal (or command prompt) and running the following commands:

```bash
java -version groovy -version
```

You should see no errors and the version numbers of the installed JDK and Groovy respectively. ### Step 4: Choose an IDE

A robust IDE enhances development efficiency. For Groovy development, the following IDEs are popular:

IntelliJ IDEA: An excellent choice that provides first-class Groovy support along with advanced features for

Java.

To install, visit the [IntelliJ IDEA website](https://www.jetbrains.com/idea/) and follow the installation instructions.

Once installed, configure the IDE to support Groovy by adding the Groovy SDK via `File -> Project Structure -> SDKs`.

Eclipse: With plugins like Groovy Development Tools (GDT), Eclipse can be used effectively to work with Groovy.

Download the [Eclipse IDE](https://www.eclipse.org/) and install the Groovy Development Tools plugin from the Eclipse Marketplace.

Visual Studio Code: Lightweight and extensible, it offers Groovy support through extensions.

Install [Visual Studio Code](https://code.visualstudio.com/) and then search for the Groovy extension in the Extensions Marketplace.

Step 5: Configure Build Tools

Using a build tool can help manage dependencies and scripts more effectively. If you decide to use Gradle for building and testing your Groovy scripts:

Install Gradle: Visit [Gradle.org](https://gradle.org/install/) and follow the installation instructions.

Create a Gradle Project: Using the terminal, create a new project with the following commands:

```bash
```

```
mkdir groovy-automation cd groovy-automation gradle
init --type basic
```

```
` ` `
```

Add Groovy Plugin: Open the `build.gradle` file and add the Groovy plugin:

```
` ` `groovy plugins {
id 'groovy'
}
repositories { mavenCentral()
}
dependencies {
implementation 'org.codehaus.groovy:groovy-all:3.0.9' //
Check for the latest version
}
` ` `
```

With your development environment set up for Groovy automation, you are now ready to start scripting and automating tasks. From seamlessly integrating with existing Java codebases to leveraging rich libraries available on the Java platform, Groovy stands out as a powerful tool for automation workflows. In the following chapters, we will delve deeper into writing effective Groovy scripts, best practices, and real-world automation scenarios. Happy coding!

Chapter 2: Groovy Fundamentals

In this chapter, we will explore the foundational concepts of Groovy, including its syntax, data types, control structures, closures, and more. Understanding these fundamentals will equip you with the tools needed to leverage Groovy's full potential in your programming endeavors.

2.1 Introduction to Groovy

Groovy was introduced in 2003 as a scripting language that would make Java development easier and more productive. Its seamless integration with existing Java code allows developers to use Groovy alongside Java, fostering an environment where both languages can thrive. Groovy introduces several features that simplify coding, such as a dynamic type system, syntactic sugar for common constructs, and support for closures.

2.1.1 Installation and Setup

To begin programming in Groovy, you need to install the Groovy environment. It can be added to your system in several ways:

Direct Download: You can download the latest version of Groovy from the [Groovy website](https://groovy-lang.org/download.html) and follow the installation instructions for your operating system.

Using SDKMAN!: SDKMAN! is a tool that makes managing parallel versions of multiple Software Development Kits easy. You can install Groovy simply by running:

```bash
sdk install groovy
```

Gradle/Maven Integration: If you are using Gradle or Maven for your projects, you can include Groovy as a dependency in your build configuration.

Once installed, you can verify your installation by running the following command in your terminal:

```bash
groovy -version
```

2.2 Basic Syntax

Groovy has a syntax that is easy to read and write, heavily influenced by Java but with several enhancements. Below, we will cover the basic syntax elements.

2.2.1 Comments

Groovy supports both single-line and multi-line comments:

```groovy
// This is a single-line comment
/*
This is a multi-line comment
*/
```

2.2.2 Variables and Data Types

In Groovy, you can define variables using the `def` keyword or by specifying the type:

```groovy
def name = "John Doe" // String int age = 30     // Integer
double salary = 75000.00 // Double
```

Groovy is dynamically typed, which means you don't need to specify the type of a variable explicitly unless you want to. This allows developers to write less boilerplate code.

2.2.3 Closures

One of Groovy's most powerful features is its support for closures, which are blocks of code that can be executed at a later time. Closures can take parameters, returning values, and are defined using the `{}` syntax:

```groovy
def greet = { name -> "Hello, $name!" }
println(greet("Alice")) // Outputs: Hello, Alice!
```

2.3 Control Structures

Like other programming languages, Groovy provides various control structures that allow you to manage the flow of your application.

2.3.1 Conditional Statements

Groovy uses `if`, `else if`, and `else` statements similar to Java:

```groovy
def x = 20
if (x < 10) {
    println("Less than 10")
} else if (x > 10) {
    println("Greater than 10")
} else {
    println("Equal to 10")
}
```

2.3.2 Loops

Groovy supports both traditional loops and enhanced loops:

```groovy
// Traditional for loop
for (int i = 0; i < 5; i++) {
    println(i)
}
// Enhanced for loop
def numbers = [1, 2, 3, 4, 5]
numbers.each { number ->
    println(number)
}
```

2.3.3 Switch Statement

The `switch` statement allows you to execute different parts of code based on the value of a variable:

```groovy
```

```
def day = "Monday" switch (day) {
case "Monday":
println("Start of the week") break
case "Friday":
println("End of the week") break
default:
println("Midweek")
}
```

2.4 Collections

Groovy has powerful built-in support for collections, such as lists, maps, and ranges, making data manipulation straightforward.

2.4.1 Lists

Lists in Groovy are dynamic arrays that can hold elements of any type:

```groovy
def fruits = ["Apple", "Banana", "Cherry"] fruits.each {
fruit -> println(fruit) }
```

2.4.2 Maps

Maps are key-value pairs that provide fast lookups:

```groovy
def person = [name: "Alice", age: 28]
println(person["name"]) // Outputs: Alice
```

```
```

2.4.3 Ranges

Ranges allow you to define a sequence of values conveniently:

```groovy
def range = 1..5

println(range.collect { it * 2 }) // Outputs: [2, 4, 6, 8, 10]
```

2.5 Exception Handling

Robust applications require proper error handling. Groovy simplifies exception handling using `try`, `catch`, and `finally` blocks:

```groovy
try {

def result = 10 / 0

} catch (ArithmeticException e) { println("Cannot divide by zero!")

} finally {

println("Execution completed.")

}
```

Groovy's rich set of features and intuitive syntax makes it a powerful language for both scripting and full- fledged application development. In this chapter, we've covered the essential elements of Groovy, laying the groundwork for more advanced topics. As you continue your journey with Groovy, try to apply these fundamentals in practice, and prepare for the exciting capabilities that lie ahead in the subsequent chapters.

Basic Syntax and Structure of Groovy

Designed to be both powerful and user-friendly, Groovy supports both static and dynamic typing, closures, and domain-specific languages (DSLs), making it a popular choice for developers looking to enhance their Java applications or create new ones from scratch.

In this chapter, we will explore the basic syntax and structure of Groovy. By understanding these fundamentals, you will be prepared to write your own Groovy scripts and applications, leveraging its features to improve productivity and code readability.

1. Groovy Basics

1.1. Installation and Setup

Before diving into the syntax, ensure you have Groovy installed on your machine. You can download it from the official website or, if you're using a package manager, install it through that. Once installed, verify your setup by running the command:

```bash
groovy --version
```

1.2. Your First Groovy Script

To get started, create a file named `HelloWorld.groovy` with the following content:

```groovy
println 'Hello, World!'
```

Run this script from the command line with:

```bash
groovy HelloWorld.groovy
```

This simple script sends "Hello, World!" to the console, demonstrating the ease of output in Groovy. ### 2. Groovy Syntax

Groovy syntax is designed to be Java-like yet more concise. Here are key components of Groovy syntax: #### 2.1. Variable Declaration

In Groovy, you can declare variables without specifying types. The language infers the type automatically.

```groovy
def name = 'John Doe' def age = 30
```

The `def` keyword is used to define a variable, and you can also use type declarations if desired:

```groovy
String name = 'John Doe' int age = 30
```

```
```

2.2. Strings

Groovy supports both single-quoted and double-quoted strings. Single-quoted strings are literal, while double-quoted strings allow for string interpolation:

```groovy
def name = 'John'

println "Hello, ${name}!" // Output: Hello, John!
```

2.3. Collections

Groovy provides several collection types, including lists and maps, which are easy to create and manipulate:

Lists:

```groovy
def fruits = ['Apple', 'Banana', 'Cherry'] println fruits[1] //
Output: Banana
```

Maps:

```groovy
def person = [name: 'John', age: 30] println
person['name'] // Output: John
```

3. Control Structures

3.1. Conditional Statements

Groovy's conditional statements are similar to Java's. You

can use `if`, `else if`, and `else` to control the flow of your program:

```groovy
def age = 20
if (age < 18) { println 'Minor'
} else if (age < 65) { println 'Adult'
} else {
println 'Senior'
}
```

3.2. Loops

Groovy provides several looping mechanisms, including `for`, `while`, and the enhanced `each` method for collections.

For Loop:

```groovy
for (int i = 0; i < 5; i++) { println i
}
```

Each Method:

```groovy
fruits.each { fruit ->
println fruit
}
```

4. Functions and Closures #### 4.1. Defining Functions

Functions in Groovy can be defined using the `def` keyword and can take parameters:

```groovy
def greet(name) {

return "Hello, ${name}!"

}

println greet('John') // Output: Hello, John!
```

4.2. Closures

Closures are a powerful feature of Groovy that allow you to define anonymous functions:

```groovy
def add = { a, b -> a + b } println add(5, 7) // Output: 12
```

Closures can also access variables from their surrounding context, allowing for elegant and flexible code. ### 5. Object-Oriented Structure

Groovy is fully object-oriented. You can define classes and create objects in a straightforward way. #### 5.1. Defining a Class

A simple class definition in Groovy looks like this:

```groovy
class Person {

String name int age
```

```groovy
String greet() {

return "Hello, my name is ${name} and I'm ${age} years old."

}


}

def john = new Person(name: 'John', age: 30) println john.greet()
```
```

In this chapter, we have covered the basic syntax and structure of Groovy. From variable declaration to control structures, functions, closures, and object-oriented programming, Groovy combines the power of Java with additional features that make coding more enjoyable and efficient. As you progress to more complex topics, you will find that mastering these basics will be crucial for effectively leveraging Groovy in your projects.

# Understanding Groovy Data Types and Variables

This chapter will delve into the data types and variables in Groovy, providing a concise yet comprehensive overview that will pave the way for effective coding practices.

## 1. Introduction to Data Types

Data types specify the type of data that a variable can hold. They define the operations that can be performed on the data and how much space it occupies in memory. Groovy,
```

being a dynamic language, simplifies working with data types by abstracting many of the complexities associated with declarative typing found in some other languages.

1.1 Dynamic Typing in Groovy

One of the defining characteristics of Groovy is its dynamic typing system. Instead of requiring developers to declare a data type explicitly, Groovy allows for dynamic assignment. This means a variable can hold different types of data at different times during program execution. For instance:

```groovy
def myVariable = "Hello, Groovy!" // Initially a String
println(myVariable)    //    Output:    Hello,    Groovy!
myVariable = 42 // Now an Integer println(myVariable)
// Output: 42
```

While dynamic typing offers flexibility, it is essential to emphasize the importance of readability and maintainability in your codebase.

1.2 Static Typing in Groovy

Despite its dynamic nature, Groovy can also operate in a statically typed manner. This is beneficial in larger applications where developers seek to enforce type safety and improve performance. Type annotations can be used as follows:

```groovy
String greeting = "Hello, Groovy!" int age = 42
```

Using static typing can be enforced with the `@TypeChecked` annotation, enabling compile-time type checking and reducing runtime errors.

2. Built-in Data Types in Groovy

Groovy provides a rich set of built-in data types that fall into two primary categories: primitive types and reference types.

2.1 Primitive Data Types

These are the simplest forms of data types that store basic values. In Groovy, the following primitive types are commonly used:

Integer: Represents whole numbers.

Double: Represents decimal numbers.

Boolean: Represents true or false values.

Character: Represents a single character (though typically used as a string).

Byte: Represents a byte value.

Short: Represents a short integer value.

Long: Represents larger integer values.

Float: Represents floating-point numbers. Example of using primitive types in Groovy:

```groovy
int number = 10

double percentage = 99.5 boolean isSuccess = true
```

2.2 Reference Data Types

Reference types store references (addresses) to objects rather than the value itself. Groovy provides several reference types, including:

String: A sequence of characters.

List: An ordered collection of elements, potentially of mixed data types.

Map: A collection of key-value pairs.

Set: A collection of unique elements. Here's an example utilizing reference types:

```groovy
String name = "Groovy" List<Integer> numbers = [1, 2, 3, 4, 5]

Map<String, String> capitals = ["USA": "Washington, D.C.", "UK": "London"] Set<String> uniqueLetters = ["A", "B", "C"]
```

3. Declaring Variables in Groovy

Declaring variables in Groovy is straightforward thanks to its dynamic nature. The keyword `def` can be used for general variable declarations, while you can specify the type for static typing.

3.1 Variable Declaration and Scope

Variables in Groovy can be declared in different scopes:

Local Variables: Defined within a method or a block and accessible only there.

Instance Variables: Associated with an instance of a class and accessible in methods of that class.

Static Variables: Defined in a class and shared across all instances of that class. Example of variable declaration within different scopes:

```groovy
class Example {
static String staticVariable = "Static"

String instanceVariable = "Instance"
void method() {
def localVariable = "Local" println(localVariable) println(instanceVariable) println(staticVariable)
}
}
```

4. Type Conversion and Type Checking

Groovy provides powerful features for type conversion and checking, especially when working with dynamic types. The language supports implicit conversion, where types can be automatically converted from one type to another.

You can explicitly convert types using methods like `.toString()`, `.toInteger()`, etc. Additionally, you can use type checking to verify whether a variable is of a specific type.

Example of type conversion:

```groovy
def number = "123"
int integerNumber = number.toInteger() // Converts String to Integer
```

And for type checking:

```groovy
if (number instanceof Integer) { println("It's an Integer!")
}
```

In this chapter, we've explored the foundations of Groovy's data types and variables, covering both dynamic and static typing, primitive and reference types, and variable declaration in various scopes. Understanding these concepts is critical for writing clear, efficient, and maintainable code in Groovy. As you continue your programming journey, keep experimenting with these features, and find the unique ways Groovy can facilitate your coding efficiency and creativity.

Chapter 3: Control Flow and Logic in Groovy

Groovy, with its flexible syntax and powerful constructs, provides a rich set of tools for managing control flow and logic. This chapter delves into the various control flow mechanisms available in Groovy, covering conditional statements, loops, and the ternary operator, along with practical examples to illustrate their usage.

3.1 Conditional Statements

Conditional statements allow programs to execute certain blocks of code based on whether a specified condition is true or false. In Groovy, the primary structures for conditional statements are `if`, `else if`, and `else`.

3.1.1 The If Statement

The `if` statement evaluates a condition and executes the associated block of code if the condition is true.

```groovy
def number = 10
if (number > 5) {
println "The number is greater than 5."
}
```

In this example, since `number` is indeed greater than 5, the output will be:

`The number is greater than 5.`

3.1.2 The Else If and Else Statements

Sometimes, you may want to evaluate multiple conditions. The `else if` and `else` statements allow you to handle additional cases.

```groovy
def number = 3
if (number > 5) {
println "The number is greater than 5."
} else if (number == 5) {
println "The number is equal to 5."
} else {
println "The number is less than 5."
}
```

Here, the output will be:

`The number is less than 5.` ### 3.1.3 Switch Statement

For situations requiring multiple condition evaluations based on a single variable, Groovy offers a convenient `switch` statement.

```groovy
def fruit = "apple"
switch (fruit) { case "banana":
println "You chose a banana." break
case "apple":
```

```
println "You chose an apple." break
default:
println "Unknown fruit."
}
```

In this situation, the output will be:

`You chose an apple.` ## 3.2 Loops

Loops are essential for executing a block of code multiple times. Groovy provides several types of loops, including `for`, `while`, and `do-while`.

3.2.1 For Loop

The `for` loop is commonly used to iterate over collections or ranges.

```groovy
for (i in 1..5) {
println "Iteration $i"
}
```

This loop will print:

``` Iteration 1
Iteration 2
Iteration 3
Iteration 4
Iteration 5
```

```
```

3.2.2 While Loop

The `while` loop continues to execute as long as the specified condition remains true.

```groovy
def count = 1
```

while (count <= 5) { println "Count is $count"

count++

}
```
```

The output will be:
```
```

Count is 1

Count is 2

Count is 3

Count is 4

Count is 5
```
```

3.2.3 Do-While Loop

The `do-while` loop is similar to the `while` loop but guarantees that the code inside the loop is executed at least once.

```groovy
```

def number = 1

```
do {
println "Number is $number" number++
} while (number <= 5)
```

output:
```

Number is 1

Number is 2

Number is 3

Number is 4

Number is 5
```

3.3 The Ternary Operator

Groovy's ternary operator provides a concise way to evaluate conditions and return results based on those conditions. The syntax follows this format:

```groovy
condition ? valueIfTrue : valueIfFalse
```

Example of the Ternary Operator

```groovy def age = 16
def status = age >= 18 ? "Adult" : "Minor" println "Status: $status"
```

Here, the output will be:

`Status: Minor`

3.4 Exception Handling

Control flow is not only about conditional execution and loops but also about handling exceptions. Groovy makes it simple to implement exception handling using the `try`, `catch`, and `finally` blocks.

Example of Exception Handling

```groovy
try {
def result = 10 / 0  // This will throw an exception
} catch (ArithmeticException e) {
println "Caught an arithmetic exception: ${e.message}"
} finally {
println "This block always executes."
}
```

The output will show:
```

Caught an arithmetic exception: / by zero This block always executes.
```

The simplicity and expressiveness of Groovy's syntax empower developers to write clean and understandable code, allowing them to focus on solving problems rather than wrestling with complex control flow logic. As we move forward, we will explore data structures and collections in Groovy, further enriching our programming toolkit.

Using Conditional Statements and Loops

This chapter delves into how you can use these constructs to make decisions and repeat actions, enabling you to build robust and flexible applications.

1. Introduction to Conditional Statements

Conditional statements allow you to execute different blocks of code based on certain conditions. In Groovy, the primary conditional statements are `if`, `else if`, and `else`. Additionally, you can use the `switch` statement for more complex conditions that involve multiple cases.

1.1 The `if` Statement

The simplest form of a conditional statement is the `if` statement. Here's the syntax:

```groovy
if (condition) {
// code to execute if condition is true
}
```

Example:

```groovy
```

```groovy
def number = 10
if (number > 5) {
println "The number is greater than 5."
}
```

In this example, the program checks if `number` is greater than 5, and if true, it prints a message. ### 1.2 The `else` Statement

You can extend the `if` statement with an `else` clause, which executes an alternative block of code when the condition is false.

Example:

```groovy
if (number > 5) {
println "The number is greater than 5."
} else {
println "The number is 5 or less."
}
```

1.3 The `else if` Statement

For multiple conditions, use `else if` to check additional conditions.

Example:

```groovy
```

```groovy
if (number > 10) {

println "The number is greater than 10."

} else if (number > 5) {

println "The number is greater than 5 but less than or equal to 10."

} else {

println "The number is 5 or less."

}
```

1.4 The `switch` Statement

When dealing with multiple potential values for a variable, the `switch` statement simplifies the code. The syntax is as follows:

```groovy
switch (variable) { case value1:

// code for value1 break

case value2:

// code for value2 break

default:

// code if none match

}
```

Example:

```groovy
```

```
switch (number) { case 1:
println "The number is one." break
case 2:
println "The number is two." break
case 10:
println "The number is ten." break
default:
println "The number is not one, two, or ten."
}
```

2. Introduction to Loops

Loops are essential for executing a block of code multiple times without requiring repetitive code writing. Groovy supports several types of loops: `for`, `while`, and `do-while`.

2.1 The `for` Loop

The `for` loop iterates over a range of values or an iterable collection. #### Example:

```groovy
for (i in 1..5) {
println "Iteration: $i"
}
```

In this loop, `i` takes on values from 1 to 5, and the code block prints the current iteration number. ### 2.2 The Enhanced `for` Loop

Groovy simplifies iteration through collections with the enhanced `for` loop. #### Example:

```groovy
def fruits = ["Apple", "Banana", "Cherry"]
for (fruit in fruits) { println "I like $fruit"
}
```

2.3 The `while` Loop

The `while` loop continues executing as long as the specified condition is true. #### Example:

```groovy
def count = 1
while (count <= 5) { println "Count is: $count" count++
}
```

2.4 The `do-while` Loop

Similar to the `while` loop, but it guarantees that the loop's body executes at least once. #### Example:

```groovy
def number = 1

do {

println "Current number: $number" number++

} while (number <= 5)
```

3. Practical Applications of Conditional Statements and Loops

Now that we understand the syntax and usage of conditional statements and loops, let's explore some practical scenarios where these constructs can be combined effectively.

3.1 User Input and Validation

You can use loops and conditionals to validate user input effectively. #### Example:

```groovy
def input

do {

println "Please enter a number between 1 and 10:" input = System.console().readLine()

} while (input.isInteger() == false || input.toInteger() < 1 || input.toInteger() > 10)

println "You entered a valid number: $input"
```

3.2 Generating a Multiplication Table

48

Loops can also be used to generate outputs like a multiplication table. #### Example:

```groovy
def number = 5
for (i in 1..10) {
println "$number x $i = ${number * i}"
}
```

These constructs enable you to create dynamic and interactive applications by making decisions and repeating tasks efficiently. With practice, you can combine these features to handle more complex programming scenarios, leading to more sophisticated and efficient code. As you continue your Groovy journey, mastering these tools will significantly enhance your programming prowess.

Writing Effective Error Handling and Debugging Code

This chapter delves into writing robust error handling and debugging code in Groovy, a powerful language that runs on the Java platform and is known for its simplicity and expressiveness. Understanding how to leverage Groovy's features for error management can significantly enhance the quality of your applications.

1. Understanding Exceptions in Groovy

Before diving into error handling, it's important to grasp

how Groovy handles exceptions. Like Java, Groovy categorizes exceptions into two main types: checked and unchecked exceptions.

Checked Exceptions: These exceptions must be either caught or declared in the method signature. Example: `IOException`.

Unchecked Exceptions: These exceptions do not require explicit handling. Example:

`NullPointerException`.

Groovy's flexibility allows developers to handle exceptions gracefully, providing better control over the program flow and debugging process.

1.1 Throwing Exceptions

You can throw exceptions in Groovy using the `throw` keyword. Here's a simple example:

```groovy
def divide(int a, int b) { if (b == 0) {

throw    new    IllegalArgumentException("Denominator cannot be zero.")

}

return a / b

}
```

In this example, attempting to divide by zero results in an `IllegalArgumentException`, clearly signaling a logic error.

2. Catching Exceptions

Capturing exceptions is achieved using the `try-catch` block, similar to Java. However, Groovy introduces a more elegant syntax that enhances readability. Here's how you can structure a `try-catch` block effectively:

```groovy
try {
def result = divide(10, 0) println "Result: $result"
} catch (IllegalArgumentException e) {
println "Caught an exception: ${e.message}"
}
```

In the above code, an attempt to divide by zero triggers the catch block, and the exception message is printed without crashing the program.

2.1 Multiple Catch Blocks

Sometimes, you may want to handle different types of exceptions differently. Groovy allows multiple catch blocks:

```groovy
try {
// Some risky operation
} catch (IllegalArgumentException e) { println "Illegal argument: ${e.message}"
} catch (ArithmeticException e) {
println "Arithmetic error: ${e.message}"
} catch (Exception e) {
```

```groovy
    println "General error: ${e.message}"
}
```

2.2 Finally Block

A `finally` block can be added to a `try-catch` structure to execute code irrespective of whether an exception was thrown. This is useful for resource management:

```groovy
try {
// code that may throw an exception
} catch (Exception e) {
println "Exception: ${e.message}"
} finally {
println "This will always execute."
}
```

3. Custom Exceptions

In Groovy, creating custom exception classes is straightforward and can help in making your error handling richer and more meaningful:

```groovy
class CustomException extends Exception {
CustomException(String message) {
super(message)
}
}
```

```groovy
// Usage
def riskyOperation() {
throw new CustomException("Something went wrong!")
}
try {
riskyOperation()

} catch (CustomException e) {
println "Caught CustomException: ${e.message}"
}
```

Custom exceptions can convey specific problems that are unique to your application, making debugging easier.

4. Logging Errors

Effective debugging depends on good logging practices. Groovy integrates well with logging frameworks like SLF4J and Log4j. Here's a simple logging example using SLF4J:

```groovy
import org.slf4j.Logger
import org.slf4j.LoggerFactory
class Example {
private static final Logger logger = LoggerFactory.getLogger(Example.class)
def doSomething() { try {
```

```
// Code that might fail
} catch (Exception e) { logger.error("An error occurred:",
e)
}
}
}
```
` ` `

Logging allows developers to keep track of errors in production environments without exposing sensitive error details to end-users.

5. Debugging Techniques

When working with Groovy, debugging can often be facilitated by various techniques and tools: ### 5.1 Console Output

Simple `println` statements can aid in debugging by tracking the flow of execution and variable states. However, remember to remove or comment them out in the production code.

5.2 Using a Debugger

Most modern Integrated Development Environments (IDEs) like IntelliJ IDEA and Eclipse support integrated debuggers. Set breakpoints and watch variables as your code executes step-by-step to pinpoint issues.

5.3 Unit Testing

Robust unit tests can reveal potential errors before they escalate. Groovy's testing framework, Spock, allows for writing expressive and comprehensible tests.

```groovy
import spock.lang.Specification

class MyServiceTest extends Specification {
def "should throw exception on invalid input"() { when:
divide(10, 0)
then: thrown(IllegalArgumentException)
}
}
```

By understanding how to utilize exceptions, logging, and debugging techniques, you can enhance the reliability and maintainability of your applications. With these practices, not only can you create resilient software, but you can also streamline the development process, ensuring smoother project delivery and a better overall user experience.

Chapter 4: Automating File Manipulation with Groovy

In the world of software development and system administration, file manipulation is a common yet critical task. Whether you're dealing with configuration files, log files, or data files, knowing how to automate these operations can save considerable time and reduce the likelihood of human error. In this chapter, we will explore how the Groovy programming language can be employed to automate file manipulation tasks effectively.

Introduction to Groovy

Groovy is a versatile language that runs on the Java Virtual Machine (JVM). It is known for its seamless integration with Java, dynamic capabilities, and concise syntax. Groovy scripts can be easily executed in a variety of environments, making it an excellent choice for automating tasks such as file manipulation. Its rich set of built-in methods for working with files allows developers and administrators to manipulate data easily.

Setting Up Groovy

Before diving into file manipulation, ensure you have Groovy installed on your machine. You can download it from the official Groovy website or use a package manager like SDKMAN! or Homebrew for the installation process. Once installed, you can run Groovy scripts directly from the command line or integrate them into larger Java applications.

To verify the installation, you can open your terminal and run:

```bash
groovy -version
```

If successful, you should see the installed version of Groovy. ## Reading Files

Reading files is often the first step in file manipulation. With Groovy, reading the contents of a file is straightforward. You can use the `File` class or Groovy's syntactic sugar to simplify file reading operations.

Example: Reading a Text File

```groovy
def file = new File('example.txt')

def content = file.text // reads the entire file as a String

println content
```

In this example, we create a `File` object pointing to 'example.txt'. The `text` property reads the contents into a String, which can then be printed or processed as required.

Handling Exceptions

When working with files, it's crucial to handle potential exceptions, such as missing files or read permissions. Groovy's `try-catch` blocks make error handling straightforward:

```groovy
try {
def file = new File('example.txt') if (!file.exists()) {
```

```
    throw new FileNotFoundException("File does not exist!")
}
def content = file.text println content
} catch (IOException e) {
println "An error occurred: ${e.message}"
}
```

Writing Files

Creating and writing to files is just as simple as reading them. Groovy provides various methods to write data to files, whether you're creating a new file or appending to an existing one.

Example: Writing to a File

```groovy
def file = new File('output.txt') file.write('Hello, Groovy!')
// overwrites the file
```

In the above example, if 'output.txt' already exists, its contents will be replaced by 'Hello, Groovy!'. If you want to append to the file instead, you can use the `withWriterAppend` method:

```groovy
file.withWriterAppend            {           writer           ->
writer.writeLine('Appending a new line...')
}
```

Manipulating File Content

Once you've read the file content, you may want to manipulate it. Groovy's powerful string manipulation capabilities make this easy.

Example: Transforming File Content

Assume you have a text file with a list of names and you want to convert them to uppercase and save the results back to a new file:

```groovy
def inputFile = new File('names.txt')

def outputFile = new File('names_uppercase.txt')

inputFile.eachLine { line ->

outputFile << line.toUpperCase() + '\n'

}

```

In this script, `eachLine` iterates over each line in 'names.txt', converts it to uppercase, and appends it to 'names_uppercase.txt' with a newline character.

Advanced File Operations

Groovy also supports more advanced file operations, such as file renaming, moving, and deleting. Let's explore a couple of these functions.

Renaming a File

To rename a file, you can use the `renameTo()` method:

```groovy
```

```groovy
def oldFile = new File('old_name.txt') def newFile = new File('new_name.txt')

if (oldFile.renameTo(newFile)) { println "File renamed successfully."

} else {

println "Failed to rename the file."

}
```

Deleting a File

Deleting files is equally straightforward. However, always ensure you want to delete the file, as this action cannot be undone:

```groovy
def fileToDelete = new File('delete_me.txt')

if (fileToDelete.delete()) {

println "File deleted successfully."

} else {

println "File was not found or could not be deleted."

}
```

In this chapter, we explored the essentials of automating file manipulation using Groovy. From reading and writing files to handling exceptions and executing advanced operations, Groovy's features make it a powerful ally for developers and administrators alike. As you practice these techniques, you'll find numerous opportunities to integrate Groovy file manipulation into your daily workflows, enhancing both efficiency and effectiveness in managing files.

Reading, Writing, and Modifying Files

In modern programming, handling files is an essential skill. Whether you're processing data, generating reports, or storing application logs, the ability to read from and write to files is crucial. Groovy, with its ease of use and concise syntax, makes file manipulation even more straightforward. In this chapter, we will explore how to read, write, and modify files in Groovy, providing practical examples to illustrate each concept.

6.1 Overview of File Handling in Groovy

Groovy integrates seamlessly with the Java I/O API, inheriting all the powerful capabilities for file manipulation. Key classes include `File`, `BufferedReader`, `BufferedWriter`, and `PrintWriter`. However, Groovy also simplifies these classes' functionality, enabling us to perform file operations with less boilerplate code.

6.1.1 The File Class

The `File` class is the foundation of file handling in Groovy. It represents a file or directory path in the file system and provides methods for various operations, such as checking if a file exists, creating files, and deleting them.

6.1.2 Reading and Writing Files

Groovy offers several concise ways to read from and write

to files. You can manipulate text files easily by utilizing Groovy's built-in methods, allowing you to focus on the content rather than the underlying implementation details.

6.2 Reading Files

Reading files in Groovy can be accomplished in a few different ways. Depending on your requirements, you can read the entire contents of a file at once or read it line by line. Let's explore a few approaches for file reading.

6.2.1 Reading Entire File Content

To read the entire content of a file into a string, you can use the `text` property.

```groovy
def file = new File('example.txt') def content = file.text

println content
```

This code snippet creates a `File` object with the specified filename and retrieves the complete file content using the `text` property.

6.2.2 Reading Line by Line

For cases where you want to process each line individually, Groovy provides a convenient way using `eachLine`.

```groovy
def file = new File('example.txt') file.eachLine { line ->
println line
}
```

In this example, `eachLine` iterates over each line in the file, allowing you to execute any operation on each line.

6.2.3 Buffered Reading

For very large files, it can be more efficient to read the file in a buffered manner. This can reduce memory usage by processing smaller chunks of data at a time.

```groovy
def file = new File('largeExample.txt') file.withReader {
reader ->
reader.eachLine { line -> println line
}
}
```

Using `withReader`, Groovy handles the resource management for you, ensuring that the reader is closed after processing.

6.3 Writing Files

Writing data to files is equally straightforward. Groovy allows you to write text or binary data efficiently. ### 6.3.1 Writing Text to a File

You can create or overwrite a file by using the `text`

property.

```groovy
def file = new File('output.txt') file.text = 'Hello, Groovy World!'
```

If you want to append data to an existing file rather than overwrite it, you can use the `append` method.

```groovy
def file = new File('output.txt') file.append('Appending this line.\n')
```

6.3.2 Writing Line by Line

To write multiple lines to a file, it can be more convenient to use `withWriter`.

```groovy
def file = new File('lines.txt') file.withWriter { writer ->


writer.writeLine('First    line.')    writer.writeLine('Second line.') writer.writeLine('Third line.')

}
```

Using `withWriter`, Groovy ensures that the writer is closed automatically, helping to manage system resources effectively.

6.4 Modifying Files

Modifying files generally involves reading the content, making changes in memory, and then writing the content back to the file. Below is a simple example of modifying a file by replacing specific text.

6.4.1 Example: Updating File Content

Suppose we want to replace every occurrence of "Groovy" with "Groovy is awesome" in a file.

```groovy
def file = new File('example.txt')

def updatedContent = file.text.replaceAll('Groovy', 'Groovy is awesome') file.text = updatedContent
```

This example reads the file's content, performs the replacement, and writes the updated content back to the file.

6.4.2 Using Temporary Files

For more complex modifications, you may want to read content, modify it, and then write it to a new file to preserve the original. Here's how you can do that:

```groovy
def file = new File('example.txt')

def tempFile = new File('temp_example.txt')

file.eachLine { line ->

tempFile.append(line.replaceAll('Groovy', 'Groovy is awesome') + '\n')

}
```

```
//     Optionally    rename    temporary    file
tempFile.renameTo(file)
```
```

This method maintains the integrity of the original file during the modification process.

In this chapter, we explored how to read from, write to, and modify files using Groovy. The built-in capabilities of Groovy streamline file manipulation tasks, allowing you to focus on the logic of your application rather than the intricacies of file handling. By understanding these essential file operations, you can enhance your applications' data processing functionalities and improve overall performance.

## Automating Folder and File Operations

Whether you are processing large data sets, handling logs, or organizing various types of files, automating these tasks can save time, reduce errors, and enhance productivity. Groovy, a powerful and flexible scripting language built on the Java platform, provides robust capabilities for automating file and folder operations.

This chapter explores how to leverage Groovy's features to streamline these operations effectively. ## Getting Started with Groovy

Before diving into file and folder operations, ensure you have Groovy installed on your system. You can check if Groovy is installed by running the following command in your terminal:

```bash

groovy --version
```

If Groovy is not installed, you can easily download it from the official [Groovy website](https://groovy- lang.org/). Once installed, you can run Groovy scripts from the command line or using an Integrated Development Environment (IDE) that supports Groovy.

Basic File Operations

Groovy makes it easy to perform basic file operations such as reading, writing, and deleting files. Let's look at some examples:

Reading a File

To read a file, you can use the `File` class and its methods. Here's how to read the contents of a simple text file:

```groovy
def filePath = 'example.txt' def file = new File(filePath)

if (file.exists()) { file.eachLine { line ->

println line

}

} else {

println "File not found: $filePath"

}
```

In this example, we create a `File` object pointing to `example.txt` and use the `eachLine` method to read and print each line from the file.
```

Writing to a File

Writing to a file is just as straightforward. You can either create a new file or append content to an existing one:

```groovy
def outputFilePath = 'output.txt' def content = 'Hello, Groovy!'
// Create or overwrite the file
new File(outputFilePath).write(content)
// Append content to the file
new File(outputFilePath).append('\nThis is an appended line.')
```

This script creates or overwrites `output.txt` with the content "Hello, Groovy!" and then appends another line.

Deleting a File

To delete a file, use the `delete` method as shown below:

```groovy
def fileToDelete = new File('fileToDelete.txt')
if (fileToDelete.exists()) { fileToDelete.delete()
println "${fileToDelete.name} has been deleted."
} else {
println "File not found: ${fileToDelete.name}"
}
```

```
```

This snippet checks for the existence of `fileToDelete.txt` and deletes it if it exists. ## Folder Operations

Folders are just as important when managing files. Groovy provides convenient methods to create, list, and delete directories.

Creating a Directory

Creating a directory can be done using the `mkdir` method:

```groovy
def dirPath = 'newDirectory'

def dir = new File(dirPath) if (!dir.exists()) {

dir.mkdir()

println "Directory created: $dirPath"

} else {

println "Directory already exists: $dirPath"

}
```

This example checks if the directory `newDirectory` exists and creates it if it does not. ### Listing Files in a Directory To list all the files within a directory, you can use the `listFiles` method:

```groovy
def directory = new File('someDirectory')

if (directory.exists() && directory.isDirectory()) {
directory.listFiles().each { file ->
```

```groovy
println file.name
}
} else {
println "Directory not found: ${directory.path}"
}
```

Deleting a Directory

To delete a directory, you first need to ensure that it is empty:

```groovy
def dirToDelete = new File('directoryToDelete')
if (dirToDelete.exists() && dirToDelete.isDirectory()) { def files = dirToDelete.listFiles()
if (files.length == 0) { dirToDelete.delete()
println "Directory deleted: ${dirToDelete.path}"
} else {
println "Directory is not empty: ${dirToDelete.path}"
}
} else {
println "Directory not found: ${dirToDelete.path}"
}
```

This code snippet checks if the directory is empty before attempting to delete it. ## Advanced File Operations

Once you are comfortable with basic operations, you can move on to more advanced topics like search and file manipulation.

Searching for Files

You can search for files using Groovy's built-in methods. Here's an example that searches for files with a specific extension in a directory:

```groovy
def searchDirectory = new File('searchDirectory') def extension = '.txt'

if (searchDirectory.exists() && searchDirectory.isDirectory()) {
searchDirectory.eachFileMatch( ~/.*${extension}$/ ) {
file ->
println "Found: ${file.name}"
}
} else {

println "Directory not found: ${searchDirectory.path}"
}
```

This code searches for all `.txt` files in `searchDirectory` and prints their names. ### Moving and Renaming Files

To move or rename a file, you can use the `renameTo` method:

```groovy
```

```
def oldFile = new File('oldName.txt') def newFile = new
File('newName.txt')

if (oldFile.exists()) { oldFile.renameTo(newFile)

println "File renamed from ${oldFile.name} to
${newFile.name}"

} else {

println "File not found: ${oldFile.name}"

}
```
```

Automating file and folder operations using Groovy can greatly enhance the efficiency of your workflows. By leveraging the built-in methods and capabilities of the language, you can easily manage files, organize directories, and perform complex operations with minimal code. In this chapter, we explored fundamental file and folder operations, as well as advanced techniques for searching, moving, and deleting files.
```

Chapter 5: Groovy for API Integration

Groovy, a dynamic language for the Java platform, offers a flexible and concise way to work with APIs, making it an ideal choice for developers looking to streamline their integration efforts. This chapter explores how to leverage Groovy for API integration, discussing its core concepts, syntax, and practical examples.

5.1 Understanding APIs

Before diving into Groovy's capabilities, we need to understand what an API (Application Programming Interface) is. APIs provide a set of rules and protocols that allow different software applications to communicate with each other. They can be RESTful (Representational State Transfer) or SOAP (Simple Object Access Protocol), with REST being the more popular choice among modern web services.

5.1.1 RESTful API Basics

REST APIs use standard HTTP methods to perform operations on resources. The primary methods include:

GET: Retrieve data from a server.

POST: Send data to a server to create a new resource.

PUT: Update an existing resource.

DELETE: Remove a resource from the server. ## 5.2 Why Choose Groovy for API Integration?

Groovy presents several advantages for API integration tasks:

Conciseness: Groovy's syntax is less verbose than Java's, allowing developers to write more expressive code with fewer lines.

Dynamic Typing: Groovy is dynamically typed, which means fewer type declarations are necessary, enabling rapid development.

Built-in JSON and XML Support: Groovy includes built-in libraries for handling JSON and XML, making it easier to parse and generate data structures commonly used in APIs.

Seamless Java Interoperability: Groovy runs on the JVM, allowing easy integration with existing Java libraries and frameworks.

5.3 Setting Up Your Groovy Environment

Before you start coding, you need to set up your development environment. Follow these steps:

Install Groovy: Download the latest version of Groovy from the [Groovy website](https://groovy-lang.org/download.html) and follow the installation instructions.

IDE Configuration: While you can use any text editor, IDEs like IntelliJ IDEA or Eclipse with Groovy support enhance productivity through features such as syntax highlighting and autocompletion.

5.4 Making HTTP Requests in Groovy

In Groovy, making HTTP requests is straightforward thanks to its built-in `HttpBuilder` library. This section covers how to perform basic HTTP operations.

5.4.1 Importing Required Classes

To start, you will need to import the `HttpBuilder`

classes:

```groovy
@Grab(group='org.codehaus.gpars', module='gpars',
version='1.2.1') import groovyx.net.http.RESTClient

import groovyx.net.http.ContentType import
groovyx.net.http.Method
```

5.4.2 Performing a GET Request

Let's perform a GET request to a public API that provides
information about users. We will be using the
JSONPlaceholder API, a simple fake REST API for testing
purposes.

```groovy
def client = new
RESTClient('https://jsonplaceholder.typicode.com/')

def response = client.get(path: 'users/1', contentType:
ContentType.JSON)

if (response.status == 200) {

println "User: ${response.data.name}"

} else {

println "Error: ${response.status}"

}
```

5.4.3 Performing a POST Request

To create a new resource, you can perform a POST request with the following code:

```groovy
def newUser = [ name: 'John Doe', username: 'johndoe',
email: 'johndoe@example.com'
]
def postResponse = client.post( path: 'users',
body: newUser,
requestContentType: ContentType.JSON
)
if (postResponse.status == 201) {
println "Created User ID: ${postResponse.data.id}"
} else {
println "Error: ${postResponse.status}"
}
```

5.4.4 Error Handling

API interactions can fail for various reasons. Implementing error handling is crucial for robust integration. Here's how to handle potential exceptions in your API calls:

```groovy
try {
def response = client.get(path: 'users/1', contentType: ContentType.JSON) if (response.status == 200) {
println "User: ${response.data.name}"
```

```
}
} catch (groovyx.net.http.ResponseParseException e) {
println "Failed to parse response: ${e.message}"

} catch (java.net.UnknownHostException e) { println
"Network error: ${e.message}"

}
```

5.5 Consuming SOAP APIs with Groovy

While REST APIs dominate the current landscape, you may still encounter SOAP APIs. Groovy can also handle these with the help of additional libraries such as Apache CXF.

5.5.1 Setting Up Apache CXF

To use SOAP services, you need to add the CXF dependencies to your project:

```groovy
@Grab(group='org.apache.cxf', module='cxf-rt-frontend-jaxws', version='3.4.4') @Grab(group='org.apache.cxf', module='cxf-rt-transports-http', version='3.4.4') import org.apache.cxf.jaxws.JaxWsProxyFactoryBean
```

5.5.2 Calling a SOAP Service

```groovy
def factory = new JaxWsProxyFactoryBean()
factory.serviceClass = MySoapServiceInterface.class
factory.address = 'http://example.com/soap-service'
```

```
def client = factory.create()
def response = client.mySoapMethod(param1, param2)
println "Response: ${response}"
```

Groovy simplifies API integration with its expressive syntax and dynamic capabilities. Whether you are consuming REST or SOAP services, Groovy provides developers with robust tools to build seamless connections between applications. In this chapter, we explored how to make HTTP requests, handle responses, and manage exceptions effectively. As you continue to delve into Groovy, you'll discover even more techniques to enhance your API integration tasks.

Sending HTTP Requests and Consuming APIs

Understanding how to send HTTP requests and consume APIs effectively is essential for modern software development. Groovy, an agile and dynamic language for the Java Virtual Machine (JVM), offers a concise and flexible way to work with web APIs. This chapter will walk you through the fundamentals of sending HTTP requests using Groovy and consuming APIs effectively.

1. Understanding HTTP and APIs

Before diving into code, it's important to grasp the concepts of HTTP and APIs:

HTTP (Hypertext Transfer Protocol): A protocol used for communication on the web. It defines methods (GET,

POST, PUT, DELETE) that are used to perform actions on web resources.

API (Application Programming Interface): A set of rules and protocols for building and interacting with software applications. RESTful APIs, which often use HTTP, are commonly used to enable communication between client and server.

2. Setting Up Groovy Environment

To start working with Groovy, ensure you have the following:

Java Development Kit (JDK): Groovy runs on JVM, so you need JDK installed.

Groovy SDK: You can download it from the official Groovy website or install it via SDKMAN, Homebrew, or other package managers.

IDE: Use any IDE that supports Groovy, such as IntelliJ IDEA or Eclipse. ## 3. Sending HTTP Requests in Groovy

Groovy simplifies the process of sending HTTP requests. The `@Grab` annotation allows you to include dependencies dynamically without adding them to your build file explicitly. For HTTP requests, we'll use the [HTTP Builder](https://github.com/restlet/restlet-framework-java) library, or for modern applications, we might utilize the `HttpURLConnection` or `groovy-wslite` module.

3.1 Using HttpBuilder

First, let's add the HTTP Builder dependency using the `@Grab` annotation.

````groovy
@Grab(group='org.codehaus.gpars',      module='gpars',
version='1.2.1')    @Grab(group='org.codehaus.httpclient',
module='httpclient',                    version='4.5.13')
@Grab(group='org.restlet.jre',          module='restlet',
version='2.3.12')

import groovyx.net.http.RESTClient

def          client          =          new
RESTClient('https://jsonplaceholder.typicode.com/')

// Sending a GET request

def response = client.get(path: '/posts/1')

println "Response: ${response.status}" println "Body:
${response.data.title}"
````

In this example, we're sending a GET request to a
placeholder API that returns fake JSON data. The
response includes the status code and the data retrieved.

3.2 Sending POST Requests

Sending a POST request is also straightforward using
`HttpBuilder`.

````groovy
def postResponse = client.post( path: '/posts',

body: [title: 'foo', body: 'bar', userId: 1],
requestContentType: 'application/json'
)

println "POST Response: ${postResponse.status}" println
````

"Body: ${postResponse.data.id}"
```

In this case, we're creating a new resource by sending a JSON body. The `requestContentType` specifies the type of data being sent.

## 4. Handling Responses

API responses can vary widely. Here's a basic approach to handle different response codes.

```groovy
try {
def response = client.get(path: '/posts/1')
switch (response.status) { case 200:
println "Success: ${response.data}" break
case 404:
println "Resource not found." break
case 500:
println "Server error." break
default:
println "Unexpected response: ${response.status}"
}
} catch (Exception e) {
println "An error occurred: ${e.message}"
}
```

This approach allows for graceful handling of various
```

HTTP status codes, enabling your application to react accordingly.

5. Advanced Usage - Consuming a Real API

To demonstrate the full capabilities of Groovy in consuming APIs, let's interact with a more complex API, such as a weather service. Suppose you have an API from a weather provider where you need an API key.

5.1 Example with an API Key

```groovy
@Grab(group='org.codehaus.gpars', module='gpars', version='1.2.1') @Grab(group='org.codehaus.httpclient', module='httpclient', version='4.5.13')

def apiKey = 'YOUR_API_KEY' def cityName = 'London'

def client = new RESTClient('http://api.openweathermap.org/data/2.5/')

def weatherResponse = client.get(path: 'weather', query: [q: cityName, appid: apiKey]) if (weatherResponse.status == 200) {

println "Weather in ${cityName}: ${weatherResponse.data.weather[0].description}"

} else {

println "Error: ${weatherResponse.status}"

}
```

In this example, we are getting weather data for London

using an API key. Make sure to replace `'YOUR_API_KEY'` with a valid API key.

We started with basic GET and POST requests, learned to handle different types of responses, and looked at how to manage real-world API scenarios. Groovy's concise syntax and built-in features make it an excellent choice for interacting with web services, allowing developers to focus on the logic without getting bogged down in boilerplate code.

Handling JSON and XML Responses with Groovy

In this chapter, we will explore how to effectively work with JSON and XML data formats using Groovy, a powerful scripting language that runs on the Java platform and is recognized for its ease of use and flexibility.

1. Introduction to JSON and XML ### 1.1. What is JSON?

JavaScript Object Notation (JSON) is a lightweight data interchange format that is easy to read and write for humans and easy to parse and generate for machines. It is built on two structures:

A collection of name/value pairs (often realized as an object).

An ordered list of values (often realized as an array).

JSON has become the standard for APIs and web services due to its simplicity and ubiquity. ### 1.2. What is XML?

eXtensible Markup Language (XML) is a markup language that defines a set of rules for encoding documents in a format that is both human-readable and machine-readable. XML facilitates the representation of complex data structures and supports a wide range of data types. While JSON has become more popular in recent years, XML remains a fundamental technology, particularly in legacy systems and for certain applications like SOAP-based web services.

2. Setting up the Groovy Environment

Before diving into handling JSON and XML responses, you'll need to set up your Groovy environment. You can download Groovy from the [official Groovy website](https://groovy-lang.org/download.html) and follow the installation instructions for your operating system.

Once installed, ensure that you can run Groovy scripts from the command line. You can check by executing:

```bash
groovy -version
```

3. Handling JSON Responses ### 3.1. Parsing JSON

Groovy provides built-in support for JSON parsing through the `groovy.json.JsonSlurper` class. To illustrate how to parse JSON, let's consider a simple example:

```groovy
import groovy.json.JsonSlurper

def jsonString = '''{ "name": "John Doe", "age": 30,
```

```groovy
"isEmployee": true,
"skills": ["Java", "Groovy", "JavaScript"]

}'"
def jsonSlurper = new JsonSlurper()
def jsonObject = jsonSlurper.parseText(jsonString)
println "Name: ${jsonObject.name}" println "Age: ${jsonObject.age}"
println "Is Employee: ${jsonObject.isEmployee}" println "Skills: ${jsonObject.skills.join(', ')}"
```

3.2. Generating JSON

Creating JSON from Groovy objects can be done using the `groovy.json.JsonBuilder` class. Here's how to create a JSON structure:

```groovy
import groovy.json.JsonBuilder
def builder = new JsonBuilder() builder {
name 'Jane Doe' age 28 isEmployee false
skills ['Python', 'Groovy', 'Ruby']
}
def jsonOutput = builder.toPrettyString() println jsonOutput
```

3.3. Making HTTP Requests with JSON

85

In many cases, you will need to make HTTP requests to retrieve JSON data. Groovy simplifies this with the `@Grab` annotation to include libraries such as `HttpBuilder`.

```groovy
@Grab('org.codehaus.gpars:gpars:1.2.1')
import groovyx.net.http.RESTClient

def client = new RESTClient('https://api.example.com/')
def response = client.get(path: '/users', query: [limit: 10])

if (response.status == 200) {

def jsonResponse = response.data

println "Fetched users: ${jsonResponse.users}"

} else {

println "Failed to fetch users: ${response.status}"

}
```

4. Handling XML Responses ### 4.1. Parsing XML

Groovy simplifies XML parsing with the `groovy.util.XmlSlurper` class. Let's look at an example of parsing XML:

```groovy
import groovy.xml.XmlSlurper

def xmlString = '''<user>

<name>John Doe</name>

<age>30</age>
```

```
<isEmployee>true</isEmployee>
<skills>
<skill>Java</skill>
<skill>Groovy</skill>
<skill>JavaScript</skill>
</skills>
</user>'''
def xmlSlurper = new XmlSlurper()
def xmlObject = xmlSlurper.parseText(xmlString)
println "Name: ${xmlObject.name.text()}" println "Age: ${xmlObject.age.text()}"
println "Is Employee: ${xmlObject.isEmployee.text()}"
println "Skills: ${xmlObject.skills.skill.collect { it.text() }.join(', ')}"
```

4.2. Generating XML

Creating XML from Groovy objects can be done using `groovy.xml.MarkupBuilder`. Here's an example:

```groovy
import groovy.xml.MarkupBuilder
def writer = new StringWriter()
def xmlBuilder = new MarkupBuilder(writer)
xmlBuilder.user { name 'Jane Doe' age 28 isEmployee false skills {
```

```
skill 'Python' skill 'Groovy' skill 'Ruby'
}
}
def xmlOutput = writer.toString() println xmlOutput
```

4.3. Making HTTP Requests with XML

Just like with JSON, you may need to handle XML data from HTTP responses. Here's a basic example:

```groovy
groovy @Grab('org.codehaus.gpars:gpars:1.2.1') import groovyx.net.http.RESTClient

def client = new RESTClient('https://api.example.com/')

def response = client.get(path: '/users/xml', query: [limit: 10])

if (response.status == 200) {

def                 xmlResponse                 =                 new XmlSlurper().parseText(response.data)

println "Fetched users: ${xmlResponse.user.collect { it.name.text() }}"

} else {

println "Failed to fetch users: ${response.status}"

}
```

In this chapter, we have explored how to handle JSON and XML responses using Groovy. From parsing and generating data formats to making HTTP requests, Groovy's syntactic simplicity and powerful built-in libraries make it a great choice for developers working with web APIs and data interchange formats. By mastering these techniques, you will enhance your ability to integrate and interact with various services in your applications effectively.

Chapter 6: Scripting with Groovy in System Operations

This chapter delves into the fundamentals of Groovy, its advantages for system operations, and practical applications that can streamline processes and improve productivity.

The Power of Groovy

Groovy is a dynamic language that builds upon the strengths of Java while introducing features that assist in rapid development. With a syntax that is both concise and intuitive, Groovy enables developers and system administrators to write scripts that are readable and maintainable. Some key features of Groovy include:

Seamless Java Integration: Since Groovy is built on the JVM, it allows for easy integration with Java libraries, facilitating the reuse of existing code.

Dynamic Typing: Groovy's dynamic typing system permits developers to write less boilerplate code, making it quicker to develop and iterate.

Built-in Support for Collections: Groovy provides powerful collection manipulation features, making it easier to manage lists, maps, and other data structures relevant to system operations.

Domain-Specific Language (DSL) Capabilities: Groovy's flexible syntax allows the creation of DSLs, making it ideal for domain-specific tasks in system management.

Setting Up Groovy

Before diving into Groovy scripting, it's essential to have a proper setup. Here's a brief guide to getting started:

Installation: Groovy can be easily installed via SDKMAN, Homebrew, or by downloading pre-built binaries. For example, using SDKMAN:

```bash
curl -s "https://get.sdkman.io" | bash

source "$HOME/.sdkman/bin/sdkman-init.sh" sdk install groovy
```

IDE Support: Although you can write Groovy scripts in any text editor, using an Integrated Development Environment (IDE) like IntelliJ IDEA or Eclipse with Groovy plugins can enhance productivity through features like code completion and syntax highlighting.

Hello World: Test your installation with a simple script. Create a file named `HelloWorld.groovy` with the following content:

```groovy
println 'Hello, World!'
```

Run the script using the command:

```bash
groovy HelloWorld.groovy
```

Groovy Basics for System Operations ### Variables and Data Types

Groovy supports dynamic typing, which allows you to define variables without explicitly declaring their types. You can use `def` for a general declaration or specify types as needed.

```groovy
def greeting = "Hello, System Admin!" int count = 5
```

Control Structures

Groovy's control structures mimic those of Java, making them familiar to most developers. Here's an example of an `if` statement and a `for` loop:

```groovy
if (count > 0) {

println "$greeting You have $count tasks to complete."

}

for (int i = 1; i <= count; i++) { println "Task $i"

}
```

Collections

Working with collections is straightforward in Groovy. You can create and manipulate lists and maps easily:

```groovy
```

```groovy
def servers = ['server1', 'server2', 'server3'] servers.each {
server ->

println "Deploying to $server"

}

def config = [db: 'mysql', port: 3306]

println "Database: ${config.db}, Port: ${config.port}"
```
```

## Practical Applications of Groovy in System Operations
### Scripted Automation

One of the primary advantages of Groovy in system operations is its capacity for automation. For instance, consider a scenario where you need to back up server configurations. A Groovy script can traverse directories, read configuration files, and archive them as follows:

```groovy
def backupDir = "/backup/configs" def configDir = "/etc/myapp/configs"

new File(configDir).eachFile { file -> if (file.name.endsWith('.conf')) {

def backupFile = new File(backupDir, file.name) file.withInputStream { input ->

backupFile.withOutputStream { output -> output << input

}

}

println "Backed up ${file.name} to ${backupFile.path}"
```
```

```
}
}
```
` ` `

Domain-Specific Language (DSL)

Groovy's capability to create DSLs means you can craft scripts that closely reflect the problem domain. For example, if you need to define server configurations, you might create a DSL that simplifies your script:

```groovy
servers {
server('server1') { ip '192.168.1.1'
role 'web'
}
server('server2') { ip '192.168.1.2'
role 'db'
}
}
```

Integrating Groovy with Build Tools

Groovy is extensively used with build and automation tools like Gradle, which is based on Groovy syntax. Leveraging Groovy in build scripts can streamline tasks such as:

Dependency management

Plugin integration

Custom task definitions

An example of a simple Gradle build script is below:

```groovy
```groovy plugins { id 'java'
}
repositories { mavenCentral()
}
dependencies {
implementation                    'org.springframework:spring-core:5.0.9.RELEASE'
}
task myTask { doLast {
println 'Running my custom task!'
}
}
```
```

With its ease of use, dynamic nature, and seamless integration with Java, Groovy allows system administrators to write scripts that are both effective and elegant. As organizations increasingly lean on automation to scale their operations, mastering Groovy will undoubtedly enhance your scripting capabilities and operational efficiency. The next chapter will explore advanced Groovy features and how they can further optimize system operations.

Running Shell Commands and Executing Scripts

Groovy, a powerful scripting language that runs on the Java platform, provides seamless ways to achieve this functionality. This chapter explores how to run shell commands and execute scripts within Groovy, covering basic uses, error handling, and best practices.

1. Understanding Groovy's Process API

Groovy has built-in support for executing shell commands through its `Process` API. This allows developers to run external processes, interact with them, and retrieve their output. The `Process` API provides a simple and intuitive way to execute system commands from within Groovy.

1.1. Creating a Process

To run a shell command, you can simply use Groovy's `execute()` method. This method can be called on a string that represents the shell command.

```groovy
def command = "ls -l"

def process = command.execute()

// Read the output

def output = process.text println output
```

1.2. Working with Input and Output Streams

When executing a command, we often want to capture both standard output and standard error. Groovy makes it easy to work with these streams:

```groovy
def command = "ls -invalidOption" def process =
```

command.execute()

// Capture the output

def output = process.inputStream.text def error = process.errorStream.text

process.waitFor() // Wait for the process to finish println "Output: $output"

println "Error: $error"

```
```

In the example above, we attempt to list a directory using a command that contains an invalid option, which results in an error. We print both the output and the error to get a complete picture of what happened.

2. Running Scripts

Groovy supports executing scripts written in Groovy or other scripting languages, such as Python or Bash. This can be accomplished in a similar manner to executing shell commands.

2.1. Executing Groovy Scripts

Suppose you have a Groovy script saved as `script.groovy`. You can execute it from another Groovy script as follows:

```groovy
def script = "groovy script.groovy" def process = script.execute() process.waitFor()

def output = process.inputStream.text println output
```

```
```

2.2. Executing Other Scripts

For other types of scripts, such as Python or Bash, the process is similarly straightforward. Just ensure that the necessary interpreter for the script is installed and accessible in your system's PATH.

```groovy
def pythonScript = "python3 your_script.py" def process = pythonScript.execute() process.waitFor()

def output = process.inputStream.text println output
```

3. Handling Errors and Exit Codes

When running shell commands or scripts, it is essential to handle errors gracefully. One method to do this is to check the exit code of the command after execution. A non-zero exit code typically indicates an error.

```groovy
def command = "mkdir new_directory" def process = command.execute() process.waitFor()

if (process.exitValue() == 0) {

println "Command executed successfully."

} else {

println "Command failed with exit code: ${process.exitValue()}" println "Error: ${process.errorStream.text}"

}
```

```
```

4. Best Practices

When interacting with the shell, there are some best practices to keep in mind:

Sanitize Input: Never run shell commands with unsanitized input from users to prevent command injection vulnerabilities.

Use a Timeout: Long-running processes can block your application. Consider using a timeout to avoid indefinite waiting.

```groovy
def command = "some_long_running_command" def process = command.execute()

// Use a timeout mechanism

if (!process.waitFor(5, TimeUnit.SECONDS)) { process.destroy() // Timeout reached, destroy the process println "The command took too long to complete."

}
```

Logging: Log outputs and errors for better debugging and monitoring of the system commands you're executing.

Running shell commands and executing scripts in Groovy is not only effective but also opens up many possibilities, from automation to system administration tasks. With Groovy's `Process` API, executing commands is straightforward, and with proper error handling, you can ensure that your applications remain robust. By following best practices, you can leverage the power of shell commands safely and effectively in your Groovy applications.

Automating System Tasks with Groovy Scripts

As organizations strive to improve productivity and minimize human errors, scripting languages such as Groovy have become invaluable tools for system administrators and developers alike. Groovy, a powerful and agile language for the Java platform, embodies the best features of dynamic languages while still leveraging the robust libraries and frameworks of Java.

This chapter will delve into the basics of Groovy scripting, how it can be applied to automate system tasks, and best practices for efficient script development. By the end of this chapter, you'll have a practical understanding of how Groovy can enhance your workflow and streamline system administration tasks.

What is Groovy?

Groovy is an object-oriented programming language for the Java platform that enhances Java by adding features from languages like Python and Ruby. With its seamless integration with Java, Groovy allows developers to use existing Java libraries while benefiting from a more concise and expressive syntax. Groovy can be utilized for various tasks, including building domain-specific languages, testing, and, importantly, automation of system tasks.

Key Features of Groovy

Dynamic Typing: Unlike Java, Groovy allows dynamic typing, making it simpler to write code without the need for verbose declarations.

Closures: Groovy supports closures—blocks of code that can be assigned to variables or passed as parameters—allowing for powerful functional programming techniques.

Easy XML Handling: Groovy simplifies XML manipulation, which is beneficial for tasks involving configuration or data exchange.

Interpolation: Groovy offers string interpolation, making it quick to create dynamic strings. ## Setting Up Groovy Environment

Before diving into script writing, proper setup is essential. Here's how to configure your environment:

Install Java: Ensure you have the Java Development Kit (JDK) installed. Groovy runs on the Java platform, so having Java installed is a prerequisite.

Download Groovy: Go to the official Groovy website and download the latest stable release. Follow the installation instructions specific to your operating system.

Set Up Environment Variables: Add Groovy's `bin` directory to your PATH variable to execute Groovy commands from the command line.

Verify Installation: Open your command line interface and type `groovy -version`. If installed correctly, it will display the version of Groovy installed.

Writing Your First Groovy Script

101

Let's start with a simple script that demonstrates Groovy's syntax and capabilities. Create a new file named `HelloWorld.groovy`.

```groovy
println "Hello, World!"
```

To run this script, navigate to your script's directory in the command line and execute:

```bash
groovy HelloWorld.groovy
```

If everything is set up correctly, you should see "Hello, World!" printed on the console. ## Automating System Tasks

With a basic understanding of Groovy, we can move on to more practical applications—automating system tasks. Groovy's capabilities shine in environments where routine tasks need to be executed frequently or where error minimization is critical.

Common Use Cases

File Operations: Automating file creation, deletion, or modification.

Monitoring System Performance: Collecting metrics such as CPU usage, memory consumption, etc.

Configuration Management: Modifying application configurations programmatically.

Database Operations: Automating database queries, updates, and migrations. ### Example: File Backup Automation

Let's create a script that automatically backs up a directory.

```groovy
def sourceDir = new File("/path/to/source/directory") def backupDir = new File("/path/to/backup/directory")

if (!backupDir.exists()) { backupDir.mkdirs()
}
sourceDir.eachFile { file ->

def backupFile = new File(backupDir, file.name) file.withInputStream { inputStream ->

backupFile.withOutputStream { outputStream -> outputStream << inputStream
}
}
println "Backed up: ${file.name}"
}
```

This script will copy all files from the specified source directory to a backup directory, creating the backup directory if it doesn't already exist.

Scheduling Groovy Scripts

To automate the execution of Groovy scripts, you can use task schedulers available on your operating system:

Windows: Use the Task Scheduler to create a task that runs the Groovy script at specified intervals.

Linux: Use the `cron` service to schedule the Groovy script by adding an entry to your crontab.

Best Practices for Groovy Scripting

Modular Code: Break scripts into functions or classes to enhance readability and reusability.

Error Handling: Implement error handling to capture and respond to exceptions appropriately.

Commenting: Use comments liberally to explain logic, especially in more complex scripts.

Testing: Regularly test your scripts in a safe environment before deploying them into production.

Version Control: Keep your scripts in a version control system like Git to track changes and collaborate easily.

Automating system tasks with Groovy scripts can significantly enhance operational efficiency and reliability. By understanding Groovy's features and adopting best practices, you can create robust automation solutions tailored to your environment. Whether it's simple file backups or more complex process automations, Groovy provides the tools and flexibility needed to manage system tasks effectively. As you explore Groovy further, you'll discover a rich ecosystem that can revolutionize the way you approach scripting and automation in your projects.

Chapter 7: Advanced Groovy Techniques for Automation

We will cover topics such as metaprogramming, domain-specific languages (DSLs), integration with tools, and performance considerations.

7.1 Metaprogramming in Groovy

Metaprogramming is one of Groovy's most potent features, allowing developers to alter the behavior of their code at runtime. Metaprogramming can help automate repetitive tasks, such as logging or input validation, without cluttering your codebase.

7.1.1 Dynamic Method Invocation

In Groovy, you can dynamically add methods to classes at runtime. This can be particularly useful in automation scripts where configuration changes often. For instance, you can create a method that reads properties from a configuration file and adds corresponding methods to a class on the fly.

```groovy
class DynamicGreeter { void greet(String name) {

println "Hello, ${name}!"

}

}

DynamicGreeter.metaClass.greetAll = { List names ->
names.each { greet(it) }

}

def        greeter        =        new        DynamicGreeter()
```

```groovy
greeter.greetAll(['Alice', 'Bob', 'Charlie'])
```

7.1.2 Intercepting Method Calls

Using Groovy's `ExpandoMetaClass`, you can intercept method calls and modify their behavior. This technique can be handy for logging and debugging, especially in automated scripts.

```groovy
ExpandoMetaClass.enableGlobally()

String.metaClass.invokeMethod = { String name, args ->
println "Invoked method: ${name} with args: ${args}"
delegate."$name"(*args)

}
println "Hello".toUpperCase()
```

7.2 Domain-Specific Languages (DSLs)

Creating a DSL in Groovy can be an effective approach for automating complex tasks, especially in areas like build scripts and configuration management. A DSL can provide a more intuitive syntax for users, allowing them to express tasks in a way that closely resembles their domain.

7.2.1 Building a Simple DSL

Let's create a simple DSL for configuring a web server with just a few lines of code. This will abstract the underlying operations and present a clean, easy-to-read format.

```groovy
```

```groovy
class ServerConfig {
String host int port
void configure(Closure closure) { closure.delegate = this
closure()
}
}
def server = new ServerConfig() server.configure {
host = 'localhost' port = 8080
}
println "Starting server at ${server.host}:${server.port}"
```

7.2.2 Using Closures for Configuration

Closures are first-class citizens in Groovy, and they can be employed effectively in DSLs. They allow for deferred execution and can encapsulate context, making configurations more modular.

```groovy
class TaskScheduler { List tasks = []
def task(String name, Closure closure) { tasks << [name: name, action: closure]
}
def run() {
tasks.each { task ->
println "Running task: ${task.name}" task.action()
}
```

```
}

}
```

def   scheduler   =   new   TaskScheduler()
scheduler.task('Backup') { println "Performing backup..." }
scheduler.task('Cleanup') { println "Cleaning up..." }
scheduler.run()
``` ` ` ` ```

7.3 Groovy and Automation Tools

Groovy integrates seamlessly with various automation tools, enhancing their functionality and enabling complex workflows.

7.3.1 Jenkins Pipeline with Groovy

Jenkins provides a powerful pipeline feature for automating CI/CD. Groovy is the backbone language for defining Jenkins pipelines, allowing you to script complex sequences of tasks.

```groovy
pipeline {

agent any stages {

stage('Build') { steps {

echo 'Building..'

}

}

stage('Test') { steps {

echo 'Testing..'

}

}
```
```

```
stage('Deploy') { steps {
echo 'Deploying..'
}
}
}
}
```
```

### 7.3.2 Ansible Playbook with Groovy

Using Groovy with Ansible can enhance your playbooks, especially when generating dynamic inventories or parameters. Groovy can generate YAML files needed for Ansible flexibility.

```groovy
def playbook = '''
- hosts: all tasks:
- name: Ensure a package is installed yum:
name: httpd state: present
'''

new File('playbook.yml').write(playbook)
```

7.4 Performance Considerations for Automation Scripts

Occasionally, automation scripts can become resource-intensive, leading to performance bottlenecks. Here are some practical suggestions to optimize your Groovy
```

scripts:

7.4.1 Optimize Looping with Closure Methods

When processing collections, use Groovy's built-in methods like `collect`, `find`, and `each`, which leverage native Java performance.

```groovy
def numbers = (1..10)

def doubled = numbers.collect { it * 2 } println doubled
```

7.4.2 Use Parallel Execution

For CPU-intensive tasks, consider leveraging parallel execution to enhance performance.

```groovy
import groovyx.gpars.*

GParsPool.withPool { (1..10).eachParallel { num ->

println "Processing number: $num"

}

}
```

From metaprogramming to domain-specific languages, and from integration with powerful tools like Jenkins and Ansible to performance optimization, Groovy offers a rich landscape of features that can streamline your automation tasks. Understanding and leveraging these features will allow you to write more effective, maintainable, and efficient automation scripts.

Using Closures, Builders, and Dynamic Typing

In this chapter, we'll dive into these three core features of Groovy, illustrating how they can enhance productivity and creativity in your coding endeavors.

1. Understanding Closures

A closure in Groovy is a block of code that can be executed at a later time. This concept is similar to a function or a lambda expression in other programming languages. Closures can take parameters, return values, and can even access variables from their surrounding scope (lexical scoping).

1.1 Creating Closures

In Groovy, you can define a closure using curly braces. Here's a simple example:

```groovy
def greet = { String name -> "Hello, $name!"
}
println greet("World") // Output: Hello, World!
```

In this example, the `greet` closure takes a single parameter and returns a greeting string. ### 1.2 Closures with Multiple Parameters

Closures can also accept multiple parameters:

```groovy
```

```
def add = { int a, int b -> a + b
}
println add(5, 10) // Output: 15
```

1.3 Closures and Context

One of the most powerful features of closures is their ability to access variables from their surrounding scope. This allows for a dynamic and flexible programming style.

```groovy
def multiplier = 2
def timesTwo = { int number -> number * multiplier
}
println timesTwo(5) // Output: 10
```

In this case, the closure `timesTwo` accesses the `multiplier` variable from its containing context.

2. The Power of Builders

Builders in Groovy provide a convenient way to create complex structures, such as XML and JSON, with a simple and intuitive syntax. Builders use closures to build up their structures, allowing for a more readable code.

2.1 Working with the MarkupBuilder

To illustrate the concept of builders, let's explore the `MarkupBuilder`, which allows us to create XML documents easily.

```groovy
import groovy.xml.MarkupBuilder
def writer = new StringWriter()
def xml = new MarkupBuilder(writer)
xml.person { name 'John Doe' age 30
address {
street '1234 Main St' city 'Anytown'
}
}
println writer.toString()
```

In this example, the `MarkupBuilder` creates a simple XML structure with embedded closures, demonstrating how easily we can generate complex outputs.

2.2 Using the JsonBuilder

Similarly, Groovy provides `JsonBuilder`, allowing us to create JSON structures with ease:

```groovy
import groovy.json.JsonBuilder
def jsonBuilder = new JsonBuilder() jsonBuilder {
person {
name 'John Doe' age 30
address {
street '1234 Main St' city 'Anytown'
```

```
}
}
}
println jsonBuilder.toPrettyString()
```
```

Like `MarkupBuilder`, `JsonBuilder` employs closures to build a well-structured output, showcasing the capabilities of builders in Groovy.

## 3. Embracing Dynamic Typing

One of Groovy's standout features is dynamic typing. This means that you do not need to declare the types of variables explicitly. Instead, Groovy infers the type at runtime, which can lead to more concise and flexible code.

### 3.1 Variable Declaration

Declaring variables in Groovy is straightforward:

```groovy
def name = "Groovy" def age = 20

println "Name: $name, Age: $age"
```

Here, `def` is used to declare variables without specifying their types. Groovy automatically infers that

`name` is a `String` and `age` is an `Integer`. ### 3.2 Methods with Dynamic Typing

Dynamic typing extends to method parameters and return types as well:

114
```

```groovy
def sum(def a, def b) { a + b
}
println sum(5, 10)   // Output: 15
println sum(5.5, 4.5) // Output: 10.0
```

In the `sum` method, we use `def` to allow for varying input types, illustrating Groovy's flexibility. ### 3.3 Duck Typing

Groovy supports a concept known as duck typing, where the type of an object is determined by its methods and properties rather than its actual class. This allows for more generic and reusable code.

```groovy
class Dog {
def speak() { "Woof"
}
}
class Cat {
def speak() { "Meow"
}
}
def communicate(def animal) { println animal.speak()
}
def dog = new Dog() def cat = new Cat()
communicate(dog) // Output: Woof communicate(cat) //
```

Output: Meow
```
```

In this snippet, the `communicate` method works with any object that has a `speak` method, leveraging the capabilities of duck typing.

Closures provide a flexible way to encapsulate logic, builders simplify the generation of structured formats, and dynamic typing allows for more adaptable code. By effectively using these features, developers can write cleaner, more maintainable, and more expressive Groovy applications. As we continue to explore more advanced topics in Groovy, these foundational concepts will serve as essential tools in your programming toolkit.

Exploring Groovy's Meta-programming Capabilities

This chapter delves into the exciting world of Groovy's meta-programming features, demonstrating how they can simplify coding tasks, enhance code flexibility, and promote more dynamic software design.

Understanding Meta-programming in Groovy

Meta-programming in Groovy is made possible through several key concepts, including the use of the

`ExpandoMetaClass`, dynamic method invocation, property manipulation, and runtime method addition. These features allow developers to alter the behavior of objects and classes on the fly, thereby enabling a more dynamic and expressive coding style.

116

1. The ExpandoMetaClass

The `ExpandoMetaClass` is one of Groovy's most powerful and dynamic features. It allows developers to add methods and properties to existing classes at runtime. This can be particularly useful when working with third-party libraries where making changes is not straightforward.

Example: Adding Methods Dynamically

```groovy
class Holiday { String name
}

def holiday = new Holiday(name: 'Christmas') println holiday.name // Output: Christmas

// Dynamically add a method to the Holiday class
holiday.metaClass.getGreeting = { -> "Merry ${delegate.name}!" } println holiday.getGreeting() // Output: Merry Christmas!
```

In this example, we see how the `getGreeting` method is added at runtime to the `Holiday` class instance, showcasing the flexibility Groovy provides.

2. Dynamic Property Access

Groovy makes it possible to dynamically access and modify properties in a very concise manner. The property syntax in Groovy is not bound to compile-time definitions, meaning you can create properties dynamically.

Example: Dynamic Property Assignment

```groovy
def person = new Expando() person.name = 'Alice'
person.age = 30 println "${person.name} is ${person.age}
years old." // Output: Alice is 30 years old.

person.gender = 'Female'

println "${person.name} is ${person.gender}." // Output:
Alice is Female.
```

In this example, we define an object `person` of type
`Expando`, allowing us to freely add properties as we
need.

3. Method Missing and Property Missing

Groovy also provides mechanisms to handle methods and
properties that do not exist. Using the

`methodMissing` and `propertyMissing` methods,
developers can create flexible and forgiving APIs. ####
Example: Handling Missing Methods

```groovy
class DynamicGreeter {

def methodMissing(String name, args) { "Hello, ${name}!"

}

}

def greeter = new DynamicGreeter()

println greeter.john() // Output: Hello, john! println
greeter.jane() // Output: Hello, jane!
```

In this example, we've created a `DynamicGreeter` class that produces a greeting for any name passed to it, even if that method wasn't explicitly defined.

4. Adding Methods to a Class

Not only can methods be added to instances, but classes can also be dynamically extended. This is accomplished using the `MetaClass` associated with the class.

Example: Extending a Class at Runtime

```groovy
String.metaClass.sayHello = { -> "Hello, ${delegate}!" }
println "Groovy".sayHello() // Output: Hello, Groovy!
```

This flexibility allows for very creative programming techniques, enabling a more fluid and expressive approach to building applications.

Practical Applications of Meta-programming ### 1. Simplifying DSL Creation

One of the most common uses for Groovy's meta-programming capabilities is in the creation of Domain-Specific Languages (DSLs). The ability to dynamically define methods and properties makes it easy to create expressive and concise syntax.

2. Mocking in Testing

Meta-programming is often used in testing frameworks like Spock, where mock objects are created dynamically with specific behaviors without having to create verbose mock classes each time.

3. AOP (Aspect-Oriented Programming)

Using Groovy's meta-programming features, developers can implement aspect-oriented patterns more easily than in many other languages. This allows for cross-cutting concerns such as logging and transaction management to be modularized effectively.

By allowing methods and properties to be defined at runtime and providing simple mechanisms for dealing with dynamic behavior, Groovy empowers developers to write cleaner, more maintainable, and flexible code. As you continue to explore Groovy, you'll find that understanding and leveraging meta-programming can significantly enhance your programming repertoire and problem-solving capabilities.

Chapter 8: Database Automation with Groovy

With its dynamic typing, closures, and built-in support for lists and maps, Groovy provides a rich set of features that simplify common programming tasks. One of its standout applications lies in database automation. In this chapter, we will explore how to use Groovy for automating database operations, including connections, queries, and data manipulation, while leveraging its capabilities to enhance productivity.

Setting Up the Environment

Before diving into database automation, it's vital to set up your environment correctly. Ensure you have the following:

Java Development Kit (JDK): Groovy runs on the JVM (Java Virtual Machine), so you'll need the JDK installed on your machine.

Groovy: Download and install the latest version of Groovy from the [official Groovy website](https://groovy-lang.org/download.html).

Database: Ensure you have access to a database system (e.g., MySQL, PostgreSQL, SQLite) and have created a sample database for experimentation.

Database Driver: Depending on your database system, download the appropriate JDBC driver and add it to your classpath.

Connecting to the Database

The first step in database automation is establishing a

connection. Groovy simplifies database interactions through the use of `Sql` class from the Groovy SQL module. Here's a basic example of connecting to a MySQL database:

```groovy
@Grab(group='mysql',    module='mysql-connector-java', version='8.0.26') import groovy.sql.Sql

def dbUrl = 'jdbc:mysql://localhost:3306/mydatabase' def user = 'root'

def password = 'password'

def sql = Sql.newInstance(dbUrl, user, password, 'com.mysql.cj.jdbc.Driver')
```

Executing SQL Queries

Once connected, you can execute SQL queries effortlessly. Groovy allows you to run SQL statements directly, either inside a transaction or as part of a batch process. Here is how to perform a simple query and process the results:

```groovy
def query = 'SELECT * FROM employees' sql.eachRow(query) { row ->

println "${row.id} : ${row.name} - ${row.position}"

}
```

In this code snippet, `eachRow` is a Groovy method that iterates over each row returned by the query, allowing you to act on each row easily.

Inserting, Updating, and Deleting Data

Automating data manipulation is a common task, and Groovy makes it straightforward. Here's how you can insert a new record into the database:

```groovy
def insertQuery = "INSERT INTO employees (name, position) VALUES (?, ?)" def params = ['John Doe', 'Developer']

sql.execute(insertQuery, params)
```

Updating and deleting records follow a similar pattern:

Update Example

```groovy
def updateQuery = "UPDATE employees SET position = ? WHERE name = ?" def updateParams = ['Senior Developer', 'John Doe']

sql.execute(updateQuery, updateParams)
```

Delete Example

```groovy
def deleteQuery = "DELETE FROM employees WHERE name = ?" def deleteParams = ['John Doe']

sql.execute(deleteQuery, deleteParams)
```

```
```

Batch Processing

When dealing with large volumes of data, performing batch operations can significantly enhance performance. Groovy allows batch processing of SQL statements efficiently. Here's how to prepare and execute a batch insert:

```groovy
def insertBatch = "INSERT INTO employees (name, position) VALUES (?, ?)" def batchParams = [

['Alice', 'Manager'],

['Bob', 'Analyst'],

['Carol', 'Designer']

]

sql.withBatch(insertBatch) { ps -> batchParams.each { params ->

ps.addBatch(params)

}

}
```

Error Handling

Error handling is crucial in any automation script to handle unexpected scenarios gracefully. Use Groovy's

`try-catch` block to manage exceptions:

```groovy try {
```

```groovy
    // Your database operations
} catch (SQLException e) {
    println "SQL Exception: ${e.message}"
} catch (Exception e) {
    println "An error occurred: ${e.message}"
} finally {
    sql.close() // Always ensure connections are closed
}
```

Closing the Connection

It's essential to close your database connections to free up resources and avoid potential memory leaks. Using the `Sql` object's `close()` method is the best practice:

```groovy
sql.close()
```

Advanced Features: Dynamic Data Manipulation

Groovy's dynamic capabilities can further enhance database automation. You can build dynamic queries based on conditions at runtime. For instance:

```groovy
def nameFilter = "John"

def dynamicQuery = "SELECT * FROM employees WHERE name = :name"

sql.eachRow(dynamicQuery, [name: nameFilter]) { row ->
    println "${row.id} : ${row.name} - ${row.position}"
```

```
}
```
```
` ` `
```

This approach allows you to customize queries based on user input or other runtime conditions without compromising security or performance.

Automating database operations with Groovy can greatly streamline workflows, enhance productivity, and reduce the chance of manual errors. By leveraging its concise syntax and powerful features, developers can transform complex database interactions into simple, manageable scripts. Whether for simple CRUD operations or more sophisticated data processing tasks, Groovy proves to be a robust solution for database automation.

Connecting to Databases and Running Queries

With its concise syntax and dynamic capabilities, Groovy makes it easier to interact with various relational databases, such as MySQL, PostgreSQL, and Oracle. In this chapter, we will explore how to connect to a database, execute SQL queries, and handle results using Groovy.

Setting Up Your Environment

Before we dive into the code, we need to ensure that our development environment is set up correctly.

Groovy Installation: Make sure Groovy is installed on your machine. You can download it from the [official Groovy website](https://groovy-lang.org/download.html).

Database Driver: Depending on the database you plan to work with, you will need the appropriate JDBC driver. Download the driver JAR file (for example, MySQL Connector/J for MySQL) and add it to your classpath.

IDE: An Integrated Development Environment (IDE) such as IntelliJ IDEA or Eclipse can make coding in Groovy much smoother, but you can also use a simple text editor and the command line.

Establishing a Database Connection

To connect to a database in Groovy, we typically use the `groovy.sql.Sql` class, which simplifies database operations. Below is an example of how to establish a connection to a MySQL database.

Example 1: Connecting to MySQL Database

```groovy
@Grab(group='mysql', module='mysql-connector-java', version='8.0.27') import groovy.sql.Sql

def dbUrl = 'jdbc:mysql://localhost:3306/mydatabase' def user = 'myusername'

def password = 'mypassword'

def sql = Sql.newInstance(dbUrl, user, password, 'com.mysql.cj.jdbc.Driver') println "Connected to the database successfully!"
```

Explanation

The `@Grab` annotation is a handy way to download

127

dependencies dynamically. It automatically downloads the MySQL driver for you.

We construct the database URL, including the hostname, port, and database name.

The `Sql.newInstance` method creates a new database connection, taking the URL, user credentials, and driver class name as parameters.

Running SQL Queries

Once connected, we can execute SQL queries using Groovy's `Sql` class. There are two primary ways to run queries: executing `execute` for updates and `eachRow` for SELECT statements.

Example 2: Executing Update and Query Statements

```groovy
// Create a new table
sql.execute('CREATE TABLE IF NOT EXISTS users (id INT PRIMARY KEY AUTO_INCREMENT, name VARCHAR(100), age INT)')

// Insert a new user
sql.execute('INSERT INTO users (name, age) VALUES (?, ?)', ['Alice', 30]) sql.execute('INSERT INTO users (name, age) VALUES (?, ?)', ['Bob', 25])

// Query the users table
sql.eachRow('SELECT * FROM users') { row ->

println "User ID: ${row.id}, Name: ${row.name}, Age: ${row.age}"
```

```
}
```
```

```

Explanation

The `execute` method can be used for tasks that change the state of the database (like creating a table or inserting records). The question mark placeholders help prevent SQL injection by separating the query from its parameters.

The `eachRow` method is specifically for SELECT queries. It iterates over the result set and allows you to access each row's data conveniently.

Handling Transactions

In scenarios where multiple operations need to be executed as a single unit, transactions are essential. Groovy allows for easy transaction management using the `Sql.withTransaction` method.

Example 3: Using Transactions

```groovy
sql.withTransaction {

try {

sql.execute('INSERT INTO users (name, age) VALUES (?, ?)', ['Charlie', 35])

// Assume some other operation that might fail

// sql.execute('SOME INVALID SQL QUERY') // Uncomment to see rollback in action

} catch (Exception e) {

println "Error occurred: ${e.message}"

// The transaction will be rolled back automatically on
```

exception

}

}

```

### Explanation

The `withTransaction` method starts a new transaction. If any operations within the block throw an exception, the entire transaction is rolled back automatically.

This is an excellent way to handle bulk operations safely.
## Closing the Connection

It's best practice to close the database connection when it's no longer needed to free up resources.

```groovy sql.close()

println "Database connection closed."

```

In this chapter, we have examined how to connect to databases and run SQL queries using Groovy. The

`groovy.sql.Sql` class simplifies database interactions, making it a powerful tool for developers. With the ability to execute CRUD operations and manage transactions, Groovy allows for efficient and effective database management.

Automating Data Updates and Maintenance
```

This is where automation comes into play. By automating data updates and maintenance, organizations can significantly improve efficiency, reduce error rates, and free up valuable resources. This chapter introduces you to automating data updates and maintenance using Groovy, a powerful language that seamlessly integrates with Java and is widely used for scripting and automation tasks.

Understanding Groovy and Its Benefits

Groovy is an agile and dynamic language that runs on the Java Virtual Machine (JVM). It offers a syntax that is both concise and expressive, making it easy to read and write. Groovy is particularly popular for its integration capabilities with Java, allowing developers to leverage existing Java libraries and frameworks while benefiting from Groovy's scripting prowess.

Key Benefits of Using Groovy for Automation:

Ease of Use: Groovy's syntax is user-friendly, which means you can write scripts quickly and with less boilerplate code compared to Java.

Integration: Groovy can interact with Java classes, making it easy to access and manipulate data stored in Java-based systems.

Scripting Capabilities: Groovy excels in writing scripts for various automation tasks, including data processing, file handling, and API interactions.

Built-in Libraries: Groovy includes numerous built-in libraries that support common tasks, such as JSON handling, XML processing, and database connections.

Common Use Cases for Data Updates and Maintenance

Automating data updates and maintenance can take many forms, depending on the nature of the data and the requirements of the organization. Some common use cases include:

Database Synchronization: Keeping data in sync across multiple databases in real-time.

Data Migration: Moving data from legacy systems to modern databases.

Scheduled Updates: Automating regularly-scheduled updates for data such as sales reports, inventory levels, or user information.

Data Cleaning: Automating the identification and correction of data inconsistencies and errors.

Batch Processing: Performing large-scale data updates in batches to improve performance and reduce downtime.

Setting Up Your Groovy Environment

Before you can automate data updates and maintenance, you'll need to set up your Groovy development environment. Follow these steps:

Install Java: Ensure you have the Java Development Kit (JDK) installed on your system.

Install Groovy: You can download Groovy from the [Groovy official website](https://groovy-lang.org/download.html). Installation instructions vary based on your operating system, so follow the documentation for setup.

Set Up an IDE: While you can write Groovy scripts in any text editor, an Integrated Development Environment

(IDE) like IntelliJ IDEA or Eclipse with Groovy support will provide helpful features such as syntax highlighting and code completion.

Automating Data Updates: A Practical Example

Let's walk through a practical example of automating data updates using Groovy. Suppose you need to update a database table with sales data from a CSV file regularly. Here's how you can accomplish this task.

Step 1: Prepare Your Data Source

Assume you have a CSV file named `sales_data.csv` with the following content:

```csv
id,product,quantity,sale_date 1,Widget A,10,2023-10-01
2,Widget B,5,2023-10-02
3,Widget C,20,2023-10-03
```

Step 2: Connect to the Database

You can use Groovy's SQL capabilities to connect to a database. Below is the code that establishes a connection to a MySQL database:

```groovy
import groovy.sql.Sql

def dbUrl = 'jdbc:mysql://localhost:3306/your_database'
def dbUser = 'your_username'

def dbPassword = 'your_password'
```

```groovy
def sql = Sql.newInstance(dbUrl, dbUser, dbPassword,
'com.mysql.cj.jdbc.Driver')
```

Step 3: Read the CSV File

Next, you'll want to read the CSV file and parse its contents. Groovy provides a simple way to read files:

```groovy
def salesData = new
File('sales_data.csv').readLines().drop(1) // Skip header
salesData.each { line ->
```

def (id, product, quantity, saleDate) = line.split(',')

```
// Pass data to the database update function
updateDatabase(sql, id, product, quantity.toInteger(),
saleDate)
```

```
}
```

Step 4: Update the Database

Now, let's define the `updateDatabase` method, which will insert or update records in the database:

```groovy
void updateDatabase(Sql sql, String id, String product, int
quantity, String saleDate) { sql.execute("""
```

INSERT INTO sales (id, product, quantity, sale_date) VALUES (?, ?, ?, ?)

ON DUPLICATE KEY UPDATE

quantity = VALUES(quantity), sale_date =

VALUES(sale_date) """, [id, product, quantity, saleDate])

```
}
```

The above SQL statement inserts a new record if it doesn't exist; otherwise, it updates the existing record. ### Step 5: Close the Database Connection

Finally, make sure to close the database connection once all updates are done:

```groovy
sql.close()
```

Scheduling Tasks for Automation

To run this script on a regular basis, you can use a scheduling tool such as Cron (on Linux) or Task Scheduler (on Windows). This way, your data updates will occur automatically, freeing you from manual intervention.

Example of a Cron Job

To schedule the script to run daily at 2 AM using Cron, you could add the following entry to your crontab:

```
0 2 * * * /path/to/groovy /path/to/your_script.groovy
```

By leveraging Groovy's powerful language features, built-in libraries, and easy database connectivity, developers can create robust automation scripts that save time, reduce errors, and enhance overall operational efficiency.

In the fast-paced world of data management, adopting automation is no longer optional—it has become a necessity for organizations striving to stay ahead in the competitive landscape.

Chapter 9: Creating Custom Libraries and Reusable Scripts

In this chapter, we will explore how to create custom libraries and reusable scripts in Groovy, enabling you to write cleaner and more maintainable code.

9.1 Understanding the Importance of Custom Libraries

Custom libraries are collections of reusable code that encapsulate common functionalities. By creating your own libraries, you can:

Promote Code Reusability: Write your code once and use it across multiple projects.

Enhance Maintainability: Make your codebase more manageable by separating concerns.

Facilitate Collaboration: Share libraries among team members, ensuring consistency across projects.

Encourage Testing: Isolate functionalities for easier testing and debugging. ## 9.2 Setting Up Your Development Environment

Before you start creating custom libraries, make sure that your development environment is set up correctly. You will need:

Groovy SDK: Ensure that you have the Groovy SDK installed on your machine.

IDE: Use an Integrated Development Environment (IDE) that supports Groovy, such as IntelliJ IDEA, Eclipse, or Visual Studio Code.

Build Tool: Familiarize yourself with a build tool like Gradle. Gradle integrates seamlessly with Groovy and will help in managing dependencies and packaging your libraries.

9.3 Creating a Simple Custom Library ### 9.3.1 Defining Your Library Structure

Start by creating a new directory for your library. A typical structure might look like this:
```

my-groovy-library/ src/

main/

groovy/

com/

example/ MyLibrary.groovy

build.gradle
```

9.3.2 Writing Your First Library Class

Let's create a simple utility class, `MyLibrary.groovy`, that provides string manipulation functions.
```groovy
package com.example


class MyLibrary {

static String reverseString(String input) { return input.reverse()

}

static String toUpperCase(String input) { return
```
138

```
input.toUpperCase()
}
}
```
` ` `

9.3.3 Configuring the Build Tool

Next, create a `build.gradle` file in the root of your library directory. This file will define how to build your library, including its dependencies and packaging options.

```
` ` `groovy plugins {
id 'groovy'
}
repositories { mavenCentral()
}
dependencies {
implementation 'org.codehaus.groovy:groovy-all:3.0.9' // specify your Groovy version
}
group 'com.example' version '1.0.0'
jar {
manifest { attributes(
'Implementation-Title':    'My    Groovy    Library',
'Implementation-Version': version
)
}
```

```
}
```
` ` `

9.4 Building and Testing Your Library

To build your library, navigate to its root directory in the command line and run:

` ` `bash gradle build

` ` `

This command will compile your Groovy files and package them into a JAR file located in the `build/libs` directory.

9.4.1 Writing Tests

To ensure the reliability of your library, you should write tests. Create a new directory called

`src/test/groovy/com/example/` and add a test class called `MyLibraryTest.groovy`.

` ` `groovy

```groovy
import spock.lang.Specification

class MyLibraryTest extends Specification { def "should
reverse the input string"() {

expect:

MyLibrary.reverseString("hello") == "olleh"

}

def "should convert the input string to uppercase"() {
expect:

MyLibrary.toUpperCase("hello") == "HELLO"

}
```

```
}
```

To run your tests, execute:

```bash
gradle test
```

9.5 Using Your Custom Library

After successfully building and testing your library, it can be consumed in other Groovy scripts or applications. Here's how to use the library in a separate Groovy script:

9.5.1 Creating a Consumer Script

Create a new script outside your library project:

```groovy
@Grab('com.example:my-groovy-library:1.0.0')    import com.example.MyLibrary

def greeting = "Hello, Groovy!"

println "Reversed: " + MyLibrary.reverseString(greeting)
println "Uppercase: " + MyLibrary.toUpperCase(greeting)
```

Using `@Grab`, you can easily include your library as a dependency. To run the script, execute the following command:

```bash
groovy MyConsumerScript.groovy
```

9.6 Best Practices for Custom Libraries

Follow Naming Conventions: Use consistent naming for classes and methods to enhance readability.

Document Your Code: Utilize Groovy's built-in support for Javadoc comments to document your library.

Version Your Library: Use semantic versioning to manage changes and compatibility.

Create Comprehensive Tests: Ensure that all parts of your library are covered by tests to prevent regressions.

Publish Your Library: Consider publishing your library to a repository like Maven Central if it's widely useful.

By following the steps outlined in this chapter, you can encapsulate functionality, share code easily, and promote best practices across your development team. As you continue your Groovy journey, remember to leverage the power of libraries, leading to cleaner, more efficient code and a smoother development experience.

Writing Modular and Reusable Groovy Code

In the world of software development, writing modular and reusable code is crucial for maintaining code quality, scalability, and ease of collaboration. Groovy, a powerful and dynamic language that runs on the Java platform, allows developers to embrace these principles with its concise syntax, dynamic features, and seamless integration with existing Java libraries.

This chapter delves into the practices and principles that lead to writing modular and reusable Groovy code. By the end of this chapter, you will understand how to structure your Groovy applications for maximum reusability and discover practical techniques to enable modular development.

1. What Does Modular and Reusable Code Mean? ### 1.1 Modular Code

Modular code refers to a design approach where functionality is broken down into smaller, self-contained

units or modules. Each module is responsible for a specific task and can be developed, tested, and maintained independently. This encapsulation makes it easier to understand and manage the codebase.

1.2 Reusable Code

Reusable code is the practice of writing components or modules that can be utilized in different parts of an application or even across multiple applications. Reusability reduces duplication and improves efficiency, allowing developers to leverage existing solutions instead of reinventing the wheel.

2. Principles of Writing Modular Groovy Code ### 2.1 Single Responsibility Principle

Every module should have a single responsibility or purpose. This principle encourages developers to create

components that do one thing well. By adhering to the Single Responsibility Principle, the code becomes more understandable and easier to test.

Implementation Example:

```groovy
```

```
class UserService {
void createUser(String username, String password) {
// Logic to create a user
}
}
class NotificationService {
void sendEmail(String email) {
// Logic to send an email
}
}
```

2.2 Open/Closed Principle

Modules should be open for extension but closed for modification. This means that while you should be able to extend the functionality of a module, you should avoid altering its existing code. This principle promotes a stable codebase and reduces the risk of introducing bugs.

Implementation Example:

```groovy
abstract class MessageSender { abstract void send(String message)
}
class EmailSender extends MessageSender { void send(String message) {
```

144

```
// Logic to send an email
}
}

class SmsSender extends MessageSender { void send(String message) {

// Logic to send an SMS
}
}
```

3. Crafting Reusable Code in Groovy ### 3.1 Use of Closures

Groovy's closures promote reusability by allowing you to create blocks of code that can be executed later. Encapsulating functionality in closures makes it easy to pass behavior and logic around.

Implementation Example:

```groovy
def processList(List items, Closure operation) { items.each { item ->

operation(item)
}
}

processList([1, 2, 3, 4]) { item -> println "Processing item: $item"
}
```

```
` ` `
```

3.2 Implementing Traits

Groovy's traits are a powerful feature that allows you to define reusable behaviors that can be mixed into classes. Traits promote code reuse without the need for deep inheritance hierarchies.

Implementation Example:

```groovy
trait Logging {

void log(String message) { println "[LOG] $message"

}

}

class UserService implements Logging { void createUser(String username) {

log("Creating user: $username")

// Additional user creation logic


}

}
```

4. Structuring Your Groovy Project for Maximum Reusability ### 4.1 Package modularization

Organize your Groovy classes into packages based on their functionality. This not only makes your codebase easier to navigate but also helps in identifying dependencies and enhancing modularity.

146

Suggested Structure:

```
``` src/
main/
groovy/
com/
myapp/
services/ UserService.groovy
NotificationService.groovy controllers/
UserController.groovy
```
```

4.2 Dependency Management

Utilize tools like Gradle or Maven to manage your dependencies. This approach not only keeps your project tidy but also allows you to easily integrate third-party libraries, enhancing the reusability of your codebase.

5. Best Practices for Reusable Groovy Code

Document Your Code: Write clear documentation for your classes and methods. This helps other developers (or your future self) understand how to use the code easily.

Create Unit Tests: Implement unit tests to ensure that your modules behave as expected. This will boost your confidence in reusing code without inadvertently introducing issues.

Follow Naming Conventions: Use descriptive names for your classes, methods, and variables. This improves code readability and helps in identifying their purpose quickly.

Encapsulate Configurations: Avoid hardcoding values inside your classes. Instead, use configuration files or external properties. This enables flexibility while reusing components in different environments.

Writing modular and reusable code in Groovy is a practice that pays dividends in both short-term and long- term projects. By adhering to the principles of modular design, embracing Groovy's features such as closures and traits, and organizing your project effectively, you can create robust applications that are easy to maintain and extend.

Packaging and Sharing Groovy Scripts

This chapter delves into the strategies and tools for packaging and sharing Groovy scripts effectively, ensuring ease of use, maintainability, and collaboration among developers.

Understanding the Essentials

Before diving into the specifics of packaging and sharing, it's essential to understand the basic principles that make Groovy scripts reusable and sharable.

Modularity: Organizing scripts into logical modules makes them easier to share and maintain. Group related functions, classes, or methods together, enhancing comprehensibility.

Dependencies: Identify external libraries or dependencies required by the scripts. Documenting these is crucial for users to set up the script properly without encountering runtime errors.

Documentation: Adding comments and creating supplementary documentation is vital. This practice not only helps you remember the purpose of each script but also aids others who may use or modify your code later.

Packaging Groovy Scripts ### 1. Using JAR Files

The most common method of packaging Groovy scripts is by bundling them into Java Archive (JAR) files. This approach encapsulates the scripts along with their dependencies, making deployment straightforward.

Steps to create a JAR file:

Ensure you have all your Groovy files organized in a designated directory.

Create a `MANIFEST.MF` file within this directory to provide metadata such as the main class or main script to execute.

Use a build tool like Gradle or Maven to compile the scripts into a JAR file. For example, with Gradle, the

`jar` task can be configured to include specific files and dependencies. ### 2. Using Groovy's Standalone Executable

Groovy also allows you to create executable scripts that can be run directly. By adding a shebang line at the top of your Groovy script, you can make it executable on Unix-like systems.

Example of a shebang:

```groovy
#!/usr/bin/env groovy
```

```
```

Don't forget to mark the script as executable:

```bash
chmod +x myScript.groovy
```

3. Creating a Groovy Module

For organizations or projects with multiple scripts, creating a Groovy module can be beneficial. This involves structuring your scripts in a way that they can be imported as a library.

Develop your Groovy classes, and place them within a package structure. This allows easy access via

`import` statements, streamlining script management and version control. ## Sharing Groovy Scripts

Once you have your Groovy scripts packaged, the next step is sharing them. Here are some approaches to consider:

1. Version Control Systems

Using version control systems (VCS) like Git makes sharing scripts not only easier but also keeps track of changes over time. Set up a repository to store your scripts, encouraging collaboration by allowing multiple users to contribute and manage versions effectively.

Common platforms for hosting Git repositories:

GitHub

Bitbucket

GitLab

2. Artifact Repositories

For larger projects, consider using artifact repositories (e.g., JFrog Artifactory, Nexus Repository) to host your packaged scripts. This helps in managing versions and dependencies efficiently and allows automated deployments.

3. Shared Libraries

If you are part of a team that frequently uses certain Groovy scripts, consider creating a shared library. This could be an internal repository that multiple projects can reference, minimizing duplication and ensuring everyone has access to the latest versions.

4. Documenting Your Scripts

While sharing scripts, bundling documentation can significantly enhance the usability of your scripts. Include:

ReadMe files detailing usage instructions, requirements, and example calls.

Annotated code with comments explaining complex logic and functions. ## Deploying and Using Shared Scripts

Once scripts are shared, the focus should shift to ease of deployment and usage. Organizations often have

continuous integration/continuous deployment (CI/CD) pipelines that can be leveraged for automating the deployment of these scripts to designated environments.

1. Continuous Integration/Continuous Deployment

Integrate your Groovy scripts into CI/CD pipelines using

tools such as Jenkins, GitLab CI, or Travis CI. This allows for automated tests and deployments, ensuring that every change is validated before being pushed into production.

2. User Training

Ensure that users of the scripts receive adequate training or resources to use them effectively. Hosting workshops or creating instructional videos can be particularly effective in disseminating knowledge.

Packaging and sharing Groovy scripts enhances collaboration, promotes reusability, and accelerates development cycles. By applying sound principles of modularity, proper documentation, and utilizing tools like version control and CI/CD pipelines, developers can create a cohesive environment where Groovy scripts thrive.

Chapter 10: Groovy in DevOps and CI/CD Pipelines

Among these tools, Groovy has emerged as a versatile and powerful scripting language that plays a significant role in DevOps practices and Continuous Integration/Continuous Delivery (CI/CD) pipelines. This chapter delves into how Groovy enhances automation, improves workflow agility, and fosters collaboration within DevOps and CI/CD environments.

10.1 Understanding Groovy

Groovy is an agile and dynamic language for the Java platform with syntax resembling that of Java, yet its capabilities are broader and more expressive. It integrates seamlessly with existing Java code and libraries, making it an excellent choice for developing scripts and applications in the realm of DevOps. Its concise syntax allows developers and operations engineers to write scripts quickly, decreasing the time between writing code and deploying it.

10.1.1 Key Features of Groovy

Simplicity and Syntax: Groovy's simple and expressive syntax allows developers to write less code that is easier to read and maintain.

Static and Dynamic Typing: Groovy supports both static and dynamic typing, giving developers flexibility in their coding practices.

Closures: Groovy supports closures, which are powerful constructs that allow functions to be treated as first-class citizens.

Integration with Java: Being built on the Java platform, Groovy can use Java libraries and frameworks without any special bridging, facilitating smooth transitions from one to the other.

10.2 Groovy in CI/CD Environments

CI/CD pipelines are critical in automating the steps of software development, from integration through delivery. By leveraging Groovy, teams can create flexible and adaptable pipelines that enhance the speed and reliability of software releases.

10.2.1 Groovy Scripts in Jenkins

Jenkins, the leading open-source automation server, is particularly notable for its integration with Groovy. Jenkins's Pipeline as Code allows teams to define their build, test, and deployment processes using Groovy- based DSL (Domain Specific Language). This approach not only promotes collaboration among team members but also allows version control over the pipeline itself.

Example: A Simple Jenkins Pipeline

Here's a minimal example of a Jenkins pipeline written in Groovy:

```groovy
pipeline {
agent any stages {
stage('Build') { steps {
```

```
echo 'Building the application...' sh 'make build'
}
}
stage('Test') { steps {
echo 'Running tests...' sh 'make test'
}
}
stage('Deploy') { steps {
echo 'Deploying the application...' sh 'make deploy'
}
}
}
}
```
```

In this example, the pipeline defines three stages—Build, Test, and Deploy—each executed sequentially. The use of the `echo` and `sh` commands allows for simple logging and shell execution, streamlining the CI/CD process.

### 10.2.2 Customizing Workflow with Groovy

The dynamic nature of Groovy allows teams to create custom logic and conditions within their pipelines. For instance, using Groovy's conditional statements and loops, teams can implement intricate workflows, adapting the pipeline based on specific parameters, such as branch names, build statuses, or environmental variables.

#### Example: Conditional Execution
```

```groovy
```groovy pipeline {
agent any stages {
stage('Build') { steps {
script {
if (env.BRANCH_NAME == 'master') { echo 'Building the
production version...'
} else {
echo 'Building the development version...'
}
}
}
}
}
}
```
```

In this example, the pipeline checks the branch name and alters the build message accordingly, demonstrating how Groovy can enhance conditional logic.

10.3 Groovy and Infrastructure as Code

In the realm of Infrastructure as Code (IaC), Groovy can be used with various tools like Jenkins Job DSL, which allows you to define Jenkins jobs programmatically. By utilizing Groovy scripts, DevOps engineers can automate the creation and configuration of Jenkins jobs, reducing manual work and minimizing human error.

10.3.1 Automating Job Creation

With Jenkins Job DSL, you can quickly create and manage jobs in your Jenkins instance using Groovy:

```groovy
job('example-job') {
scm {
git('https://github.com/example/repo.git')
}
triggers {
scm('H/5 * * * *') // Polling every 5 minutes
}
steps {
shell('make test')
}
}
```

This script defines a job that checks out code from a specified Git repository, sets up a polling trigger, and executes a shell command to run tests.

10.4 Benefits of Using Groovy in DevOps

Integrating Groovy into your DevOps practices offers a host of advantages:

Increased Productivity: Groovy's brevity and expressiveness enable faster script development, allowing teams to respond more swiftly to changing requirements.

Improved Collaboration: By using Groovy in CI/CD

pipelines, all project stakeholders can understand and contribute to the automation scripts, fostering collaboration between developers and operations teams.

Enhanced Maintainability: Groovy's syntax encourages clearer, more readable code, making it easier to maintain and extend over time.

As we navigate the complexities of modern software delivery, Groovy stands out as a powerful ally in the DevOps toolkit. By enabling customizable, maintainable, and efficient CI/CD pipelines, Groovy empowers teams to embrace automation while enhancing collaboration and productivity. As organizations continue to evolve in their software development practices, the integration of Groovy into DevOps and CI/CD strategies will undoubtedly play a pivotal role in shaping the future of software delivery.

Automating Build Processes with Groovy

Automation is the key to streamlining development workflows, and Groovy—a powerful scripting language for the Java platform—offers an elegant solution for automating build processes. In this chapter, we will explore how to leverage Groovy for building and deploying software, enhancing productivity, and minimizing errors in the build cycle.

1. Understanding Build Automation ### 1.1 What is Build Automation?

Build automation refers to the process of automatically compiling source code into executable code, packaging applications, and running tests. This goes beyond just compiling; it also includes various integrations with other tools for code quality checks, deployment, and even continuous integration and delivery (CI/CD).

1.2 Benefits of Build Automation

Consistency: Automated builds lead to consistent results across different environments.

Efficiency: Reducing manual effort allows developers to focus on coding rather than repetitive tasks.

Speed: Automated processes can significantly speed up development cycles.

Error Reduction: Less human intervention results in fewer errors in the build process. ## 2. Why Groovy?

Groovy is a versatile language that integrates seamlessly with Java, making it a popular choice for automating build processes. Here are some reasons to consider Groovy for your build automation:

Easy Syntax: Groovy's syntax is simple and concise, making it easier to write and understand scripts.

Integration with Java: As a JVM language, Groovy can utilize the vast ecosystem of Java libraries, providing powerful capabilities for developers.

Domain-Specific Languages (DSLs): Groovy provides the ability to create DSLs, enabling developers to construct build scripts in a language that closely resembles natural language.

3. Setting Up Groovy for Build Automation ### 3.1 Prerequisites

To get started with Groovy, ensure you have:

Java Development Kit (JDK) installed.

Groovy installed (can be downloaded from [groovy-lang.org](https://groovy-lang.org/download.html)).

A basic understanding of scripting in Groovy.

3.2 Creating Your First Groovy Script

Open your favorite text editor or IDE and create a script named `build.groovy`. Here's a basic example to show how Groovy syntax works:

```groovy
println 'Starting the build process...'

// Define a function to compile code def compileCode() {

println 'Compiling source code...'

}


// Call the compile function compileCode()

println 'Build process completed.'
```

This simple script demonstrates the structure of Groovy code and serves as a foundation for more complex build automation tasks.

4. Automating with Gradle ### 4.1 Introduction to Gradle

Gradle is a powerful build automation tool that uses Groovy DSL, making it a natural fit for Groovy enthusiasts. It provides a robust framework for defining tasks and dependencies, making it particularly effective for Java projects.

4.2 Setting Up Gradle To get started with Gradle:

Install Gradle from [gradle.org](https://gradle.org/install/).

Create a `build.gradle` file in your project directory.

4.3 Example Gradle Build Script

Here is an example build script that compiles Java code and runs tests:

```groovy
apply plugin: 'java'

repositories { mavenCentral()
}

dependencies {

testImplementation 'junit:junit:4.13.2'
}

task customCompile { doLast {

println 'Compiling Java code...'
}
}

task runTests(type: Test) { useJUnitPlatform()
}

build.dependsOn customCompile build.finalizedBy runTests
```

```
```

This script specifies dependencies, creates tasks, and defines relationships between different tasks, illustrating how powerful Gradle's capabilities are when combined with Groovy.

5. Advanced Build Automation with Groovy

5.1 DSL for Build Scripts

Creating DSLs in Groovy allows you to define custom scripts that are highly readable. Here's a simple example:

```groovy
class SimpleBuild { def tasks = []

def task(String name, Closure action) { tasks << [name: name, action: action]
}
void run() { tasks.each { task ->
println "Running task: ${task.name}" task.action.call()
}
}
}
def build = new SimpleBuild() build.task('compile') {
println 'Compiling code...'
}
build.task('test') {
println 'Running tests...'
```

```
}
build.run()
```
```

### 5.2 Integration with CI/CD

Automating builds using Groovy can be integrated into CI/CD pipelines using popular tools like Jenkins, GitLab CI, or GitHub Actions. Groovy scripts can trigger builds, perform unit tests, and facilitate deployments, ensuring your changes are consistently tested and deployed.

## 6. Tips for Effective Automation

**Modularize Scripts**: Break down larger scripts into smaller, reusable functions or classes.

**Error Handling**: Implement error handling to catch failures and provide meaningful feedback during the build process.

**Documentation**: Document your scripts to make them easy to understand and maintain.

**Version Control**: Store your Groovy scripts in a version control system to track changes over time.

By leveraging tools like Gradle and creating custom DSLs, developers can create powerful build systems tailored to their projects. As you delve into building automation with Groovy, you'll discover a world of possibilities that accelerate development and streamline deployment, setting the stage for a more efficient and effective software development lifecycle. Embrace the automation journey—your future self will thank you!
```

Using Groovy with Jenkins and Other Tools

With its syntax that is both expressive and easy to read, Groovy is particularly popular in the DevOps and CI/CD communities for automating tasks and scripting.

One of the most prominent tools that leverage Groovy's capabilities is Jenkins, a widely-used open-source automation server. Jenkins allows developers to build, test, and deploy their software more efficiently.

Groovy plays a crucial role in Jenkins by enabling users to write Pipeline scripts, which define the build process, as well as custom plugins to enhance Jenkins's functionalities.

Why Use Groovy with Jenkins?

Declarative Syntax: Groovy's syntax closely resembles that of Java, but it is more concise, making it easier and quicker to write build scripts.

Integration with Java: Because Groovy is built on top of the Java platform, it can seamlessly interoperate with Java libraries, allowing developers to take advantage of existing Java code.

Dynamic Nature: Groovy's dynamic nature makes it more flexible for scripting and defining behavior without static typing.

Rich Ecosystem: Groovy is supported by a robust ecosystem that includes various libraries which can be beneficial when writing Jenkins pipelines or other automation scripts.

Jenkins Fundamentals

Before diving into using Groovy, it's important to understand the basic components of Jenkins:

Jobs: A job is a single task that Jenkins executes. This can be anything from running a shell script to building a software project.

Pipelines: A pipeline is a series of steps that automate the process of building, testing, and deploying applications. Pipelines can be defined using Groovy scripts, making it easier to manage complex workflows.

Plugins: Jenkins's functionality is extensible through plugins. Many plugins utilize Groovy for configuration and custom actions.

Creating Your First Jenkins Pipeline with Groovy

To create a Jenkins pipeline using Groovy, follow these key steps:

Step 1: Install Jenkins

Ensure that you have Jenkins set up on your server. You can download it from the [official Jenkins website](https://jenkins.io/).

Step 2: Create a New Pipeline Job

Navigate to the Jenkins dashboard.

Click on "New Item."

Enter a name for your job and select "Pipeline."

Click "OK" to proceed.

Step 3: Define the Pipeline Script

In the pipeline configuration page, scroll down to the "Pipeline" section and enter your Groovy script. Here's a simple example:

```groovy
```groovy pipeline {
agent any

stages {
stage('Build') { steps {
echo 'Building...'
// Add build commands here (e.g., shell commands)
}
}
stage('Test') { steps {
echo 'Testing...'
// Add test commands here
}
}
stage('Deploy') { steps {
echo 'Deploying...'
// Add deployment commands here
}
}
}
}
```
```

```
```

This example defines a pipeline with three stages: Build, Test, and Deploy. Each stage will output text when executed.

Step 4: Save and Execute

After entering your Groovy script, click "Save" and then "Build Now" to execute your pipeline. You can monitor the progress in the Jenkins console output.

Advanced Groovy Features in Jenkins ### Using Variables and Parameters

Groovy allows you to use variables and parameters in your pipeline scripts to customize builds. Parameters can be defined in the pipeline and can take user input, making your jobs more dynamic.

```groovy
pipeline {
agent any

parameters {
string(name: 'MY_PARAM', defaultValue: 'Hello', description: 'A parameter for demonstration')
}

stages {
stage('Echo Parameter') { steps {
echo "The parameter value is: ${params.MY_PARAM}"
}
```

```
}
}
}
```

Writing Groovy Functions

You can define custom Groovy functions to encapsulate common tasks, making your scripts more modular and reusable.

```groovy
def greetUser(String name) { echo "Hello, ${name}!"
}
pipeline { agent any


stages {
stage('Greet') { steps {
script {
greetUser('World')
}
}
}
}
}
```

Integration with Other Tools

Groovy not only enhances Jenkins capabilities but can also seamlessly integrate with other tools in your CI/CD pipeline:

Gradle: Groovy is the primary language for Gradle build scripts, allowing you to manage project dependencies, build processes, and more.

Docker: Groovy can be used in Jenkins to automate Docker image builds and deployments through Docker commands.

Configuration Management Tools: Integration with tools like Ansible or Chef can be scripted in Groovy, facilitating deployments across different environments.

Best Practices for Using Groovy in Jenkins

Keep It Simple: While Groovy allows for complex scripts, keep your pipelines simple and straightforward. This makes them easier to read and maintain.

Version Control: Store your pipeline scripts in version control (e.g., Git) to track changes and collaborate with your team.

Error Handling: Implement error handling in your scripts to catch failures and provide meaningful messages or recovery actions.

Documentation: Document your Groovy scripts within the code to explain the purpose of complex logic, making it easier for others to understand.

Modular Design: Use shared libraries to create reusable functions, allowing you to maintain a cleaner and more organized codebase.

By mastering the use of Groovy in Jenkins, developers can

create powerful pipelines that not only enhance productivity but also improve code quality and reliability. As you continue to explore Groovy, consider integrating it with other tools in your CI/CD toolkit, and embrace its potential to create a more efficient and automated development workflow.

Chapter 11: Security and Best Practices in Groovy Automation

Automating tasks and processes using Groovy, a dynamic language on the Java platform, can dramatically improve efficiency and reduce the potential for human error. However, like any programming or scripting environment, Groovy automation presents specific security challenges. This chapter delineates best practices and security measures that should be implemented to ensure that your Groovy automation efforts are both effective and secure.

11.1 Understanding the Security Landscape

Before diving into best practices, it is crucial to understand the potential security risks involved in Groovy automation. Groovy scripts run on the Java Virtual Machine (JVM), which inherently exposes them to risks associated with Java applications. Common threats include:

Code Injection: Attackers can exploit vulnerabilities to execute arbitrary code by injecting malicious scripts into your Groovy automation environment.

Insecure Data Handling: If sensitive data is processed without adequate protection, it could be exposed to unauthorized users or systems.

Environment Compromise: If an automated job interacts with a variety of environments (development, testing, production), a breach in one could affect the entire ecosystem.

As we delineate strategies for mitigating these risks, it is essential to maintain a layered security approach, combining multiple practices to reinforce your Groovy automation landscape.

11.2 Best Practices for Secure Groovy Automation ### 11.2.1 Code Quality and Reviews

Implementing a robust code review process is fundamental to ensure that your Groovy scripts are secure and maintainable. Regular code reviews should focus on:

Best Coding Practices: Apply industry-standard coding practices, such as consistent naming conventions, proper error handling, and modular designs.

Static Code Analysis: Utilize tools like SonarQube or Checkstyle to automatically analyze the security and quality of your Groovy code for vulnerabilities.

11.2.2 Secure Data Management

When dealing with sensitive information, adhere to the following guidelines:

Encryption: Always use encryption (both at rest and in transit) for any sensitive data. Groovy allows integration with Java's cryptography libraries, enabling you to encrypt and decrypt sensitive information seamlessly.

Environment Variables: Store sensitive data such as API keys and passwords in environment variables rather than hard-coding them into your scripts. This practice minimizes exposure and simplifies secret management.

11.2.3 Limited Permissions and Principle of Least Privilege

Adopt the principle of least privilege by restricting permissions for execution environments:

User Roles: Ensure that accounts used to run Groovy scripts only possess the permissions necessary to perform their functions. For example, avoid giving admin access for scripts that only need read permissions.

Sandboxing: Where feasible, execute Groovy scripts in a sandboxed environment. This isolation can prevent potentially harmful actions from affecting the broader system.

11.2.4 Regular Updates and Dependency Management

Libraries and frameworks that your Groovy scripts depend upon can often introduce vulnerabilities. Adopt these best practices:

Keep Dependencies Updated: Regularly update your libraries and frameworks to mitigate exposure to known vulnerabilities.

Use Dependency Scanning Tools: Tools such as OWASP Dependency-Check or Snyk can help identify and mitigate vulnerabilities in dependencies.

11.2.5 Logging and Monitoring

A robust logging and monitoring strategy should be part of your automation framework to identify and respond to potential security incidents:

Detailed Logging: Log all actions taken by Groovy scripts, including inputs and outputs. This helps in auditing actions for any suspicious behavior.

Alerting Mechanisms: Set up alerts for abnormal

activities or errors in script execution, allowing for a swift response to potential security incidents.

11.2.6 Testing and Vulnerability Assessment

Continuous testing is crucial in identifying security flaws in your Groovy automation processes:

Unit and Integration Testing: Regularly test your scripts using unit tests to ensure they function as expected and don't introduce vulnerabilities.

Vulnerability Assessments: Schedule routine vulnerability assessments on your automation framework to identify and remediate potential security issues proactively.

11.2.7 Documentation and Training

Adequate documentation and training can foster a security-centric culture within your team:

Documentation: Maintain clear and concise documentation regarding security practices used in your Groovy automation framework, making it accessible to developers and operators.

Training: Regular training sessions on security best practices can boost a team's awareness and ability to recognize potential threats.

By following the best practices outlined in this chapter, organizations can enhance the security of their Groovy automation processes and mitigate the risk of unintended errors or malicious attacks. As technology evolves, continuous vigilance and adaptation will play vital roles in maintaining a secure automation environment, ensuring that productivity gains come without compromising security.

Avoiding Common Mistakes in Groovy Automation Scripts

However, despite its strengths, many developers encounter pitfalls that can hinder script effectiveness or lead to runtime errors. In this chapter, we will explore common mistakes made in Groovy automation scripts and provide guidance on how to avoid them.

1. Understanding Groovy's Dynamic Nature

One major allure of Groovy is its dynamic typing; however, this feature can lead to confusion if not handled carefully. Unlike statically typed languages, errors in types may not surface until runtime, which can complicate debugging.

Common Mistake: Ignoring Type Safety

Solution: Even though Groovy allows dynamic typing, consider using static type checking features or type annotations where applicable. Using the `@TypeChecked` annotation can help surface errors at compile time instead of runtime, improving overall code reliability.

```groovy
@TypeChecked
def addNumbers(Number a, Number b) { return a + b
}
```

2. Improper Variable Handling

Groovy makes it easy to create and manipulate variables, but incorrect scoping or unintended variable shadowing can wreak havoc.

Common Mistake: Shadowing Variables

Solution: Be vigilant about variable names and scopes. When dealing with closures or nested functions, always use clear and distinct variable names to prevent accidental scope shadowing.

```groovy
def processList(List items) { items.each { item ->

// Avoid using 'item' again in this context

def processedItem = item.process() // Clear naming to avoid confusion println processedItem

}

}
```

3. Overreliance on the Metaprogramming Features

Groovy provides powerful metaprogramming capabilities, but overusing them can lead to complex and hard- to-maintain code.

Common Mistake: Using Metaprogramming Excessively

Solution: Use metaprogramming judiciously. Stick to conventional programming for the majority of your code, and leverage metaprogramming only when necessary, such as when you need to dynamically create methods or access properties.

```groovy
// Example of metaprogramming class DynamicClass {
// Use carefully
def propertyMissing(String name) { return "Property $name is not defined!"
}
}
```

4. Neglecting Error Handling

Automation scripts often run unattended, making robust error handling imperative. Neglecting this aspect can lead to unexpected failures.

Common Mistake: Failing to Implement Error Handling

Solution: Always include try-catch blocks to manage exceptions gracefully. Logging the errors can also help in diagnosing failures later.

```groovy
try {
// some risky operation
} catch (Exception e) {
println "An error occurred: ${e.message}"
// Log the error for documentation
}
```

5. Inefficient Use of Collections

Handling collections in Groovy is straightforward with the multitude of helper methods provided. However, ignoring performance considerations can lead to inefficient scripts.

Common Mistake: Inefficient Looping

Solution: Use Groovy's collection methods, such as `collect`, `find`, and `each`, which are optimized for readability and efficiency.

```groovy
def squares = (1..10).collect { it * it } // Efficient and concise
```

6. Hardcoding Values

Hardcoding values can compromise the flexibility of your scripts, making them less reusable and more prone to errors when parameters change.

Common Mistake: Using Hardcoded Values

Solution: Rely on configuration files or environment variables to manage values that may change. Groovy's built-in support for reading properties from files can facilitate this approach.

```groovy
def config = new Properties()

config.load(new FileInputStream("config.properties")) def apiUrl = config.getProperty("api.base.url")
```

7. Lack of Documentation and Comments

Without proper documentation, maintenance of automation scripts can become challenging, especially in team environments.

Common Mistake: Neglecting Comments and Documentation

Solution: Invest time in commenting your code. Use meaningful variable names and include block comments where necessary to describe the purpose of complex sections.

```groovy
/**

This method processes input data and returns results.

@param inputData Data to be processed

@return Processed results

*/
def processData(inputData) {
// Logic implementation goes here
}
```

By being mindful of type safety, variable scopes, error handling, performance considerations, configurability, and documentation, developers can greatly enhance the quality of their automation endeavors. As you continue to grow in your Groovy scripting journey, remain vigilant and proactive in refining your practices to ensure successful automation outcomes. Happy scripting!

Implementing Security Best Practices in Automation

Groovy, a versatile scripting language primarily used for building automation scripts, integration tasks, and other development processes, provides a rich ecosystem to accomplish this. However, without careful consideration of security practices, automation scripts can introduce vulnerabilities that compromise systems and data. This chapter explores essential security best practices tailored for Groovy automation scripts to help ensure robust, secure deployments.

Understanding Security Risks in Automation

Before delving into best practices, it's crucial to understand the common security risks associated with automation in Groovy:

Hard-coded Secrets: Storing sensitive information such as passwords or API keys directly in scripts can lead to unauthorized access if those scripts are exposed.

Insecure Dependencies: Utilizing third-party libraries or plugins without verifying their security can introduce vulnerabilities.

Improper Input Validation: Automations that process user input without validation may be susceptible to injection attacks.

Excessive Permissions: Running scripts with unnecessary privileges can lead to exploitation if a script is compromised.

Inadequate Logging and Monitoring: Without sufficient logging, detecting and responding to malicious activities becomes challenging.

Best Practices for Secure Groovy Automation ### 1. Manage Secrets Securely

Use Environment Variables: Instead of hard-coding sensitive data, use environment variables to access credentials during runtime.

```groovy
def dbUser = System.getenv('DB_USER')

def dbPassword = System.getenv('DB_PASSWORD')
```

Utilize Secret Management Tools: Integrate secret management services such as HashiCorp Vault, AWS Secrets Manager, or similar tools to handle sensitive information securely.

2. Validate and Sanitize Inputs

Always validate and sanitize inputs received from external sources or user input. Utilize Groovy's built-in features or libraries to check data types, formats, and boundaries.

```groovy
def safeInput(String input) {
if (input ==~ /^[a-zA-Z0-9]*$/) { return input
} else {
throw new IllegalArgumentException("Invalid input!")
}
}
```

```
```

3. Use Secure Dependencies

Regularly audit and update third-party libraries to mitigate vulnerabilities in dependencies. Use tools like OWASP Dependency-Check to identify known vulnerabilities in libraries used within your Groovy scripts.

```
```groovy dependencies {

implementation                    'org.apache.commons:commons-lang3:3.12.0'

// Ensure to follow secure coding standards for each dependency

}
```
```

4. Implement Principle of Least Privilege

Set permission scopes to the minimum necessary for scripts to function. Executing scripts with higher privileges than required can lead to detrimental breaches if the script is exploited.

```
```groovy

// Consider using a limited user for executing automation scripts sh 'sudo -u limitedUser ./your-script.groovy'
```
```

5. Ensure Robust Error Handling

Implement error handling that does not expose sensitive information in logs or error messages. Use Groovy's try-catch mechanism wisely.

```groovy
try {
// Your automation task
} catch (Exception e) {
log.error("An error occurred: ${e.message}.")
// Handle exception safely without exposing sensitive data
}
```

6. Enable Logging and Monitoring

Ensure that all automation scripts have adequate logging implemented. Log execution results, errors, and environment configurations for auditing purposes. Monitor logs for any unusual activities.

```groovy
import java.util.logging.Logger


Logger logger = Logger.getLogger("AutomationLogger")
logger.info("Executing automation task...")
```

7. Regularly Update and Patch

Keep your Groovy environment and all related tools updated to their latest stable versions to protect against known vulnerabilities.

Implementing security best practices in automation scripts written in Groovy is a vital aspect of ensuring the integrity, confidentiality, and availability of applications and data. By managing secrets securely, validating inputs, using secure dependencies, adhering to the principle of least privilege, implementing robust error handling, and maintaining proper logging and monitoring, organizations can reduce the risks associated with automation and foster a culture of security-first automations.

Conclusion

As we reach the end of our journey through the world of Groovy programming, we hope you feel empowered and inspired to leverage this versatile language for automation in your own projects. Groovy's intuitive syntax, seamless integration with Java, and robust features provide a powerful toolkit for streamlining workflows and simplifying your coding experience.

Throughout this book, we've explored the fundamental principles of Groovy, from its basic syntax to its advanced capabilities. You've learned how to harness the power of Groovy scripts, utilize its dynamic features, and employ elegant approaches to automate mundane tasks. Whether you are automating build processes, integrating APIs, or managing data, Groovy stands out as an exceptional choice for enhancing productivity and efficiency.

As you venture into your Groovy programming endeavors, remember that experimentation is key. Embrace the flexibility of the language and explore its vast ecosystem of libraries and frameworks designed to extend your capabilities. The Groovy community is also a rich resource, offering forums, tutorials, and documentation that can support you at every step of your journey.

Automation is not just a trend—it's a fundamental shift in

how we approach coding and workflow management. By adopting Groovy, you are not only investing in a powerful tool but also embracing a mindset of innovation and efficiency. We encourage you to continue exploring new ways to automate and optimize your processes, and to share your experiences with others in the community.

In closing, we hope this book has provided valuable insights and practical knowledge that you can apply to your daily projects. Embrace the full potential of Groovy, and may it unlock new levels of productivity and creativity in your programming endeavors. Happy coding and automation!

Biography

Davis Simon is a passionate software developer, seasoned backend architect, and advocate for clean, efficient code. With over a decade of experience in web application development, Davis has built scalable, high-performing systems for startups and enterprises alike. His expertise lies in backend development and leveraging the power of languages like Groovy to create APIs and microservices that are as robust as they are elegant.

A self-proclaimed "Groovy enthusiast," Davis discovered the language early in his career and quickly fell in love with its versatility and simplicity. His dedication to Groovy programming inspired him to write this book and share his insights with aspiring developers looking to harness its potential for backend development.

When he's not writing code or crafting the next big web application, Davis enjoys exploring emerging technologies, mentoring new developers, and experimenting with creative ways to solve programming challenges. Outside of the tech world, Davis is an avid gamer and a lover of all things sci-fi, often finding inspiration for his projects in futuristic tales and virtual worlds.

With this eBook, Davis invites you to join him on a journey to revolutionize backend development with Groovy. His approachable teaching style and practical advice will empower you to take your skills to the next level—whether you're building your first API or architecting complex systems.

Glossary: Groovy Programming Language for Automation

A

Aggregation: The process of combining multiple data sources or elements into a single cohesive unit, often used in data processing and transformation.

API (Application Programming Interface): A set of protocols and tools that allow different software applications to communicate. In the context of Groovy, it often refers to the libraries and frameworks that Groovy can access through Java.

--- ### B

Bean: A reusable software component encapsulated in the JavaBeans conventions, often used in Groovy code to create objects that can be manipulated dynamically.

Build Automation: The process of automating the creation of executable applications from source code, which often includes compiling, linking, and packaging. In Groovy, tools like Gradle and Maven are frequently utilized.

--- ### C

Closure: A first-class function in Groovy that can be passed around as a variable and can capture variables from its surrounding scope. Closures are pivotal in Groovy for callback methods and event handling.

Continuous Integration (CI): A software development practice in which members of a team integrate their work frequently, often leveraging automated scripts written in Groovy for building and testing applications.

--- ### D

DSL (Domain-Specific Language): A programming language specialized to a particular application domain. Groovy allows developers to create DSLs that facilitate automation tasks in specific industries or frameworks.

Dynamic Typing: A feature of Groovy that allows variable types to be determined at runtime, offering more flexibility and reducing boilerplate code.

--- ### E

Enum: A special Java type used to define collections of constants. Groovy enhances enum types with additional capabilities, making them more flexible and easier to use in automation scripts.

--- ### F

Framework: A reusable set of libraries and tools that provides a structure for developing applications. In the Groovy ecosystem, popular frameworks include Grails for web applications and Spock for testing.

--- ### G

Grails: A web application framework that utilizes Groovy and is built on top of the Spring Framework. It is designed to be highly productive and follows the "convention over configuration" philosophy.

Groovy Scripts: Short pieces of code written in Groovy that perform specific automation tasks. They can be executed independently and are commonly used for tasks like system configuration or batch processing.

--- ### H

Hook: A mechanism that allows custom code to be executed at specific points in a system's process. In automation, Groovy scripts can be used as hooks to extend functionality.

--- ### I

Integration Testing: A level of software testing where individual units are combined and tested as a group. Groovy provides tools such as Spock that streamline this process.

--- ### J

Java Compatibility: Groovy is built on the Java platform and is fully compatible with Java libraries, which allows automation developers to leverage existing Java code seamlessly.

--- ### L

Lazy Evaluation: A programming technique where expression evaluation is deferred until its value is needed. Groovy supports lazy evaluation, improving efficiency in automation scripts.

--- ### M

Meta-programming: The practice of writing code that can modify or extend the behavior of other code at runtime. Groovy's meta-programming capabilities enable dynamic modifications that enhance automation workflows.

P

Pipeline: A concept in continuous delivery and integration that defines the automated path from code commit to deployment. Groovy scripts can be used to build and manage pipelines.

Property: A characteristic of an object in Groovy, typically defined using getters and setters. Properties are essential for creating configurable behaviors in automation scripts.

--- ### R

Runtime: The period during which a program is executing. Groovy scripts are executed at runtime, allowing for dynamic decision-making capabilities during automation tasks.

--- ### S

Script: A set of instructions written in Groovy

intended to be executed by the Groovy interpreter. Scripts are heavily used in automation processes for system administration, testing, or deployment tasks.

Spock: A testing and specification framework for Java and Groovy applications, allowing for expressive and powerful testing of automation scripts.

--- ### T

Test Automation: The use of software tools to create tests that can be executed automatically. Groovy is often employed in writing automated tests due to its expressive syntax and ease of integration with Java libraries.

--- ### U

Unit Testing: A software testing method where individual units of source code are tested to determine whether they are fit for use. Groovy's testing frameworks facilitate robust unit testing approaches.

--- ### V

Variable: A storage location paired with a name that holds data which can be modified during the execution of a script. Groovy offers a flexible syntax for declaring variables.

--- ### W

Workflow Automation: The process of automating complex business processes and functions beyond conventional automation. Groovy is often integrated into workflow engines to streamline processes.

X

XML (eXtensible Markup Language): A markup language used to encode documents in a format that is both human-readable and machine-readable. Groovy provides robust libraries for parsing and manipulating XML, often used in automation tasks.

--- ### Y

YAML (YAML Ain't Markup Language): A human-readable data serialization format often used for configuration files. Groovy supports YAML, making it easier to integrate configurations within automation scripts.

--- ### Z

Zip: A file format that supports lossless data compression. Groovy can manipulate zip files using its built-in capabilities to streamline automation tasks, such as packaging applications or archiving logs.